Praise for *Up Is Not the Only Way*

"This book is a refreshing take on a topic of interest to nearly everyone. Like a multifaceted dia~

—Jack Zenger, C ~ *Extraordinary*
Leader and *Sp*

"One res~ book
suggest more
comfor~

—Rosa~
Direc

"Helping ~very
level. T talk
about c

—Ken ~ *ute*
Ment

"Filled w ~es. It
teaches your
career i

—Marsl ~ *Von't*
Get Y~

"A lively, ~nark
with po ~dous
persona

—Ed Te x
Tool (

"The authors provide v ~es for meaningful career discussions."
—Tamar Elkeles, Ph~ Capital, LLC

"We have leveraged ~ a strategic talent development approa~

—Joel Tobin, Vice Pre~ ~pment, Catalent
Pharma Solutions

"This book will open ~ ~poss~ ~beyond what lies ahead—for y~ ~our org~

—Sue Padernacht, Chief L~ ~er and Vice President, Talen~ and Organization Development, Tribune Online Content

"No talent strategy can be complete without the proper attention on how employees can grow within their current organizations. Written in a practical manner, this book offers great ideas."
—**Jayne Johnson, Vice President, Global Organization and Leadership Development, Vertex Pharmaceuticals**

"This book speaks to both the employee and the manager, recognizing that a career conversation is a two-way dialogue."
—**Meribeth Germino, Principal Executive Development Consultant, Genentech**

"Today, lateral moves, stretch assignments, and career resets are all part of the lifelong journey toward professional success and personal fulfillment. This book is an invaluable tool in helping people navigate this complex new landscape."
—**Sekhar Ramaswamy, Chief Talent Officer, Prudential**

"I've found that individuals join organizations that they believe will grow their careers. This book will help everyone prepare for the development conversation and understand what it takes to own your own learning."
—**Kimo Kippen, Vice President, Global Workforce Initiatives, Hilton**

"This book helps readers understand the many ways they can grow their careers, how to evaluate their options, and what steps to take to achieve their goals."
—**Lauren Starkand, Senior Vice President, Talent and Diversity, Global Consumer Banking, Citi**

"This book provides those contemplating 'what's next?' and 'what's best for me?' with a contemporary game plan firmly grounded in the wisdom of experience."
—**Kevin D. Wilde, Executive Leadership Fellow, Carlson School of Management, and former Chief Learning Officer, General Mills**

"By enlisting individuals, their leaders, and organizations in a mindful 'think about, talk about' approach, the authors inspire positive accountability for managing careers in an uncertain world."
—**Tim Richmond, Senior Vice President, Human Resources, AbbVie**

"This is a classic 'teach them to fish' tool for thinking broadly about professional growth and building personally fulfilling, custom careers."
—**Fran Lawler, Vice President of Human Resources, Engineered Fastening, Stanley Black & Decker**

"Knowing yourself is the key to pe██████████ this book has many practical ways to accomplish that."
—**Amy Meeuwenberg, Lead Performance a██████████ent Specialist, Enterprise Talent Development, Amway**

Up is not
the only way

Other titles by the author:

Love 'Em or Lose 'Em (with Sharon Jordan-Evans)

Love It, Don't Leave It (with Sharon Jordan-Evans)

Hello Stay Interviews, Goodbye Talent Loss
(with Sharon Jordan-Evans)

Help Them Grow or Watch Them Go
(with Julie Winkle Giulioni)

Up is not the only way

Rethinking
Career Mobility

Beverly Kaye I Lindy Williams I Lynn Cowart

CAREER SYSTEMS INTERNATIONAL

BK
Berrett–Koehler Publishers, Inc.
a BK Business book

Berrett-Koehler Publishers, Inc.
1333 Broadway, Suite 1000
Oakland, CA 94612-1921
Tel: (510) 817-2277   Fax: (510) 817-2278   www.bkconnection.com

ORDERING INFORMATION

Quantity sales
Special discounts are available on quantity purchases by corporations, associations, and others. For details, contact the "Special Sales Department" at the Berrett-Koehler address above.

Individual sales
Berrett-Koehler publications are available through most bookstores. They can also be ordered directly from Berrett-Koehler: Tel: (800) 929-2929; Fax: (802) 864-7626; www.bkconnection.com

Orders for college textbook/course adoption use
Please contact Berrett-Koehler: Tel: (800) 929-2929; Fax: (802) 864-7626.

Orders by U.S. trade bookstores and wholesalers
Please contact Ingram Publisher Services, Tel: (800) 509-4887; Fax: (800) 838-1149; E-mail: customer.service@ingrampublisherservices.com; or visit www.ingrampublisherservices.com/ Ordering for details about electronic ordering.

Cataloging-in-Publication Data is available at the Library of Congress.

ISBN: 978-1-5230-8348-0

First Edition
23 22 21 20 19 18 17   10 9 8 7 6 5 4 3 2 1

Cover: Susan Malikowski, DesignLeaf Studio
Design and production: Seventeenth Street Studios
Copyeditor: Todd Manza
Proofreader: Laurie Dunne
Indexer: Richard Evans

To our children:

Lindsey and Jill

Chris, Matt, and Seamus

Shelbie and Justin

■

May you always know that up is not the only way…
but learning and loving is!

Contents

Note from the Authors

What does career advancement mean to you? What does it mean to support the career of someone who works with you? Did the image of a ladder just appear in your mind? If so, we'd like to offer some other images to reflect the workplace we all have now.

Up is not the only way. Promotions still happen. Up is still an option. But careers consist of a range of experiences—large and small—that ultimately come together to shape a career journey. Continuing to move up the ladder was never the only way or the best way or even the most satisfying way to navigate a career. For many years, though, continuous upward progression was the accepted image of a career. We offer a different image. In place of a ladder of promotions, think of career as a rich, flexible mix of experiences.

Our subtitle reads *Rethinking Career Mobility.* So what are we asking you to rethink? Careers today are mobile. That's not new. Sometimes the mobility is the traditional kind. Individuals move from function to function or take an assignment in another location. Other times, career mobility takes the form of identifying skills that are transferable from one role or profession to another.

Here's what's new. We have learned, in decades of studying careers around the globe, that career mobility can also mean growing, stretching, learning, and transforming, without ever changing the job title or even the chair you are sitting in! Career mobility is up to each individual to examine and define. I own just how mobile I will be in terms of how much, when, and how I will grow. I can create my own career patterns.

We

challenge

you to watch
for your

"I never thought of it that way before!" moments.

We will offer six experiences, six ways to grow, develop, and learn, that can be pieces of unique career patterns. How those experiences fit together over time is up to each one of us to decide.

One more thing. *Up Is Not the Only Way* is also about building a dialogue. It's about creating ongoing, two-way, formal and informal communication between individuals and their managers, coaches, mentors, and others to ensure that career experiences reach maximum potential and possibilities. We will offer ways to initiate, enrich, and engage in that dialogue. Whether the conversations are about your career, a direct report's career, or the career of a colleague or friend, you can use the questions you find in each chapter to drive your conversations deeper.

So, there you have it. The book is about building career patterns from all types of experiences, understanding what mobility means at the individual level, and engaging in dialogue that brings it all to life.

Up Is Not the Only Way is for anyone who knows, in your heart of hearts, that there are multiple ways to grow. The book is for individuals who want to learn more about how to plan and manage a career in a world of work that is in a constant state of change. The book is for managers, coaches, and mentors who are looking for ways to make career conversations more productive and focused on options. In other words, this book is for anyone who has an interest in influencing career growth—their own or that of someone else.

How you read the book is up to you. You could:

- read it and be ready for conversations with people you lead, manage, coach, counsel, or mentor.

- read it and be ready for conversations with your manager, coach, counselor, or mentor about *your* career.

- ask someone who is helping you with your career to read it so the two of you can talk about which chapters grabbed your attention and made you think.

- read it straight through, or scan the table of contents and jump in where a chapter title catches your eye.

- bring together a group of your peers to talk about the experiences the chapters describe.

- read the mobility moments scattered throughout the book then share *your* career story with others.

- pick it up whenever you have a few minutes to read a page or a chapter.

- drill down deeper at www.UpIsNot.com [password: upisnot] to access Kickstart Mobility.

Whatever approach you take, we challenge you to watch for your *I never thought of it that way before!* moments. Jot them down. Mark the page. Mind-sets change when thinking shifts.

Some estimates say we spend more than 100,000 hours working during a lifetime. We believe those hours will be more satisfying and meaningful if we feel like we are progressing in whatever way we each define progress. So, whether you are focused on your own career, helping someone else, or both, you are building a future! We welcome the opportunity to help you do it!

Bev, Lindy, and Lynn

Up is not
the only way

CHAPTER

I

UP

was never for everyone

Careers used to be PREDICTABLE.

There were **paths**

and *ladders.*

The hierarchy worked

—FOR SOME.

As downsizing, restructuring, and delayering took hold in the late 1980s, old ladders became largely inaccessible. Some rungs disappeared, and the space between others shifted from steps to leaps. At the same time, individual aspirations and company needs were evolving. Terms like *work–life balance* were overheard in break rooms. Organizations began to examine how breadth of experience weighed against depth of expertise during talent reviews. The world of work was changing.

Careers today happen in that world—a world that continues to change. The environment is more global, more multigenerational, more dispersed, diverse, and complex than ever before. Hierarchies continue to flatten. Organizational structures are flexing. Even the value people place on work is changing.

Employees play multiple roles—from individual contributor to peer to leader and back, sometimes in the same day or within the same assignment. Roles emerge and evolve based on tasks and needs. Carefully written descriptions no longer define the boundaries of a job. Teams form and disperse based on projects. Feedback comes from multiple sources. The ladder, if it's still there, may be harder to see and tougher to climb.

Is This the End of the Career as We Know It?

Every industry is changing. As a result, internal workplace structures are changing as well. Up—the promotion path and perhaps even a ladder or two—may still exist, and could still be a goal—for some. However, as levels of the hierarchy have disappeared, promotional opportunities have become less available, so the route to a promotion may take new turns. Someone who wants to manage others can still get there and, with the right mix of experiences, will likely arrive better prepared to take on the role.

Flattened organizations and limited career ladders don't spell the end of growth *or* careers. Opportunities are there—different and varied, but very much still there, and even more plentiful. The next change frontier, then, is people's mind-sets, and that means changing the conversation, especially about careers.

Let's Be Honest

Up was never for everyone. It still isn't. Managing someone else is not on everyone's radar. Neither is taking on increasing levels of responsibility (really!). Not everyone wants to move up. That doesn't mean a rewarding career is out of reach.

The message has been out there for a while now that individuals *own* their careers. What does that really mean? We think it means that the definition of career success is up to each one of us. Every time circumstances shuffle the deck, you can deal yourself a new hand. That's good news . . . actually that's *great* news! We are the only ones who can envision and imagine what success will look

Flattened organizations and **limited career ladders** don't spell the end of **growth** or **careers.**

like. And, to add to that great news, as the creators of our career success pictures, we are free to alter them when and how we choose to! *That* is what it means to *own* a career.

But, if we own it and we can create it, how do we do it?

First it's about being *mobile*.

Career Mobility . . .

. . . is essential for individuals at all levels. Each one of us needs to exercise agility and resilience that stable workplaces did not require. No longer is mobility just about physically moving to another building or town. It's more than getting promoted. It's sometimes just being willing to continue to learn and grow and stretch.

. . . is about flexibility and agility. Like the navigation systems we rely on to reroute our travels based on traffic patterns, career mobility means flexing, adapting, and anticipating what's next.

. . . involves a rich mix of experiences, roles, assignments, and options. Careers today require us to be open to exploring multiple opportunities and possibilities. Great careers will be the payoff for employees who watch for and recognize emerging growth opportunities and are ready with alternatives when options fade or change.

Second, it's about *ownershift*!

Ownershift: Who Does What?

We've all heard that employees *own* their careers. The organization needs to provide tools and resources, and managers need to support employees' career development. It's a partnership. Nothing new there!

What *is* new is talking less about the owner*ship* and more about the owner*shift*—the need to fine-tune who owns what—and about what each player needs to do to demonstrate commitment to the partnership.

Individuals must define what success means to them personally. This means testing assumptions and exploring options. It means learning and applying the insights gained from exploration. It means building plans and following through on them. It requires being a little introspective and taking time to figure things out— like what skills they have or need, what interests them, and what they value most about their work. It means asking for feedback and listening, even when it's not all good news. And, most importantly, it means being willing to take responsibility for your future. Careers belong to individuals. A career evolves within a network of partners and support, but, bottom line, it's up to the owner to shape it and live it.

The definition of career success is up to each one of us.

Managers, **coaches**, and **mentors** provide support through conversations; sharing stories; listening to individuals describe their interests, skills, and values; reacting to plans; offering feedback and connections. That support is vital to ownershift! When managers offer on-the-job learning, let's call it what it is—development. Stretch assignments are growing-in-place opportunities, not just "extra work." When someone completes a stretch assignment, taking the time to debrief it will make learning stick. *What did you learn? What skill did you acquire or sharpen? How will you apply what you learned?* The support role includes preparing individuals to learn, helping them focus on what they learned, and then guiding them to apply the new skill or capability. It's a big role, sure. And it might mean shifting what you presently think it involves, but that's

Career Mobility...

...is **ESSENTIAL**.

...is about *flexibility* and *agility*.

...involves a **rich mix** of experiences.

what we mean by ownershift. Each partner needs to understand the expectations and deliver on them.

Organizations have a role to play as well. The systems, processes, and tools the organization provides deliver on promises of a development culture. However, the organization's role doesn't end there. Through senior leadership, human resources, and related groups, the organization must ensure that employees have *access* to the tools—that employees know where to find them, what they offer, and how to use them. The organization must thread the message of development through existing communications vehicles and devise new ways to promote growth in all its shapes, sizes, and forms. Some employees tell us that their companies still celebrate only promotions—people who are moving *up*. Ownershift requires a change in that mind-set. This book can help accomplish that shift.

When the Shift Hits the Fan

We know that not everything happens as smoothly as we might like. Every organization has its own culture and unique environment. So what do you do if

. . . ownershift is just words without action?

. . . individuals are not ready?

. . . the organization isn't fully on board?

. . . some managers are just not good at this development thing?

Do you simply sit back and wait for the others to catch up? Certainly not! Whether development and growth are tracked and measured or left to chance, they are fundamental to building the future—for individuals and for organizations! Don't wait! Start now. You can start small, with a few conversations. When career conversations are happening, when individuals begin to talk about ideas and aspirations, when feedback is candid and insights emerge, everyone involved will know—*you* will know—you have completed your ownershift!

Owner*shift* is owner*ship* in *action.*

THINK ABOUT IT · · ·

At the end of each chapter we will share some questions to use as conversation starters. The questions will help you explore and build deeper dialogue about careers—yours and others'! The questions and topics will challenge you to think more broadly, whether in preparation for a conversation with your peers, with your own manager or coach, or perhaps with the leaders of your organization.

For this first chapter, here are some things for you to ponder:

* What does career success mean to you?

* How do you feel about up not being the only way?

* Considering the information in this chapter, how mobility-minded are you? What gets in your way?

* How prepared are you for an "ownershift"?

* What does growth look like for you right now?

· · · TALK ABOUT IT

CHAPTER
2

to

Kaleidoscope

Kaleidoscope

Changing
landscapes
offer unique

Turn in your telescope. Pick up your kaleidoscope. A telescope offers you one linear point of view—one straight line focused on something that may be pretty far away. A kaleidoscope gives you a fascinating array of views. Rather than having a clear, static career path, the workplace's changing landscape offers us unique patterns to view and evaluate. Like the design change even one small turn of the kaleidoscope gives you, the experiences that make up a career shift offer a wide variety of development options and a pretty amazing array of growth possibilities, including some you can reach for now—if, and *only* if, you learn to appreciate the emerging displays.

Did you know that the inside of the typical, basic kaleidoscope contains just three mirrors? Yes! All those intricate patterns can result from just three mirrors and a handful of beads or pieces of glass. Positioned at angles to one another, the mirrors combine to reflect one another as well as the items captured in the base of the tube. As beads shift and move with each twist of the kaleido-scope tube, the three mirrors produce unique patterns—patterns waiting for you to consider and act on them.

Mirror, Mirror

Like the three-mirrored kaleidoscope, there are three components that guide a satisfying career. Those three components are skills, interests, and values.

Skills include all the tools you have collected in your tool kit: those capabilities you developed in that very first job, what you

learned as you started your career journey, as well as the abilities you are polishing right now. Some of those skills might be things you hope to never have to use again. That knowledge points you to the second mirror: **interests**. Your inventory of interests includes those work tasks you like to do. You may not yet be expert in the things that interest you, but the interests mirror holds items that intrigue you enough to make the work of learning or polishing them worth it. Most people really want a chance to do what they do best.

And that third mirror? It's the one that's probably closest to your heart. The third mirror holds your **values**—those things you hold dear, things that are important to you. When you examine the values mirror, you are looking at what keeps you committed to accomplishing a task that's tough or challenging. The values mirror contains factors like "serving others," "being creative," and "spending time with family and friends"—fundamental aspects of a role or assignment that can make or break your job satisfaction.

All three mirrors matter. Understanding what's inside each one is a start. Examine your skills list: What's in your tool kit? Review your inventory of interests: What's energizing and enticing? Explore your values: What's so important that it simply must be a part of the next role or job? When you clarify what you're good at (your skills and abilities), what you enjoy (your interests), and what's important to you (your values), you've created your personal three mirrors, your *kaleidoscope*.

In combination, the three mirrors can reveal which opportunities and experiences will be the most rewarding and satisfying. Even small turns of the kaleidoscope tube can change the image and reposition which emerging opportunities will best match your mirrors. When you know what your mirrors are made of, you can make better choices about what's next in your career journey.

A Kaleidoscope View: The Basics

Here are some basics to adopting a *kaleidoscope view*.

APPRECIATE PATTERNS

As the view of careers shifts from telescope-type paths (aiming for one distant point in space) to kaleidoscope-type patterns, opportunities and options multiply. Where a path offers a singular next step, a pattern offers multiple ways to proceed, depending upon individual needs and desires, in the context of the immediate environment—ways we may never have imagined. A twist or change will produce new and sometimes different choices rather than simply shutting down a path.

A new pattern can be just as **exciting** as a former one, to the **flexible** and *agile* viewer.

With each twist of the tube, whether self-initiated or the result of external forces, you will have new patterns and new opportunities to consider.

For example, if the leadership team splits an existing department into two, options multiply. You may have had a telescope view of someday directing the old department. Now you can think about directing one of the new ones, moving laterally to direct the other, carving a new role as liaison between them. . . . When you appreciate the new pattern, you see choices.

ENCOURAGE OPTIONALITY

During an interview for this book, a client shared the term *optionality*. When asked to describe the riskiest career choice she had made in her career journey, she hesitated. She then explained that she didn't feel she had made *risky* choices—something we found surprising, considering that her choices included joining the army at eighteen, moving around between distinctly different industries, and taking two years off to go back to school! She explained that the reason she felt choices others might view as risky were not so concerning was that she always made sure she had *optionality*. She

Resilience
is built on
multiple options—
on optionality!

Good choices balance money & meaning

always had a plan A, a plan B, and a few others in her back pocket. She built resilience into her every decision.

With optionality, if plan A becomes less attractive, plans B, C, D, and more are ready and available. Eyeing career goals through a telescopic lens, zeroing in on just that dream job with the cool title and swanky office, may lead to disappointment when the title disappears or the office gets downsized. Optionality means being ready to implement any one of multiple plans when the kaleidoscope twists to produce a new landscape.

Try this idea on for size: *I don't have to leave. I could add more skills.* Could it fit you? Could it fit someone who reports to you? Turn the kaleidoscope to imagine what else is possible, right where you are.

BALANCE MONEY AND MEANING

As millennials joined the workforce they made this point crystal clear: *it's about more than just money.* Meaning has taken on an even more important role in the equation.

Hierarchies encouraged a telescope view, and the focus was often more money. Yet how many people do you know who made it to the job in their telescope and felt empty after a while, when the money couldn't keep the job shiny and exciting?

We're not suggesting that money isn't important. What we *are* suggesting is that, now more than ever, it is time to balance the scales of *money* and *meaning*.

Rather than all-or-nothing trade-offs where individuals must decide to take the money and leave meaning behind or choose to eat ramen noodles for three meals a day to have a meaningful career, we believe that finding the right balance is the key to success. We have met hundreds of people who, every day, throw their energy into work that is not paying big bucks. They probably earn enough to cover the rent or mortgage and a dinner out every now and then. But these individuals would not give up their roles of helping, serving, teaching, and learning. They know they are making contributions that are important to them, every day.

Career mobility allows you to define your own measures for balancing money and meaning, rather than accepting something prescribed by external criteria. It results in a wider range of possibilities and honors the individual. Terms like *fulfillment* and *sense of purpose* can move conversations beyond just salary and wages when examining career choices. Conversations that open all three mirrors of a personal kaleidoscope—skills, interests, and values— will result in more informed and fulfilling career options.

LOSE THE ORG CHART; BUILD AN ORB CHART

Many organizations have moved away from purely hierarchical structures to designs that accommodate a more project-based approach to work and allow for greater cross-functional relationships. The information technology industry led the way with the introduction of the "agile" approach, where individuals move quickly between or within teams, switching assignments, exchanging roles, and interfacing with multiple colleagues to tackle an array of challenges. Talent orbits one team or assignment, then moves to another, and another, as needs change and projects

Orbiting

builds **flexibility**
and moves **expertise**
to where it's needed most.

end. Employees take with them an ever-expanding inventory of knowledge, experience, and connections. The insights they gain will help them make even more valuable contributions in the future. Imagine how orbiting can enhance the ability to manage others, if and when the time comes.

These agile experiments have shown us that traditional organizational structures beg for a new view: careers that play out in new, flexible structures and offer rich career experiences. Perhaps the organization charts of the future will be flexible orbiting images that depict a workplace where individuals move about, orbit around colleagues depending upon the task at hand, and then move on.

> Not long ago, the Career Systems International leadership team took on the task of updating our organization chart. It seemed like a straightforward, get-it-done kind of chore—until we got started. We quickly realized that the tidy hierarchical set of boxes connected by straight and right-angled lines simply wouldn't work. CSI teams don't fit nicely into that model. We move around from project to project, some short term, some longer; we orbit into projects as needed and then move on. We are not alone in working this way.

Nimble organizations and agile individuals are already embracing this model. Orbiting models of work will result in even more career mobility patterns.

These new views of career development have everything to do with the way we see and navigate growth opportunities.

Instead of a telescopic perspective that presents a linear path, shifting workplace structures require us to widen our view, to align career development with the changing environment, to look around us to see what possibilities exist. A kaleidoscope view of career mobility provides many scenarios and multiple opportunities, based on whether the tube twists left or right, the time before a new pattern emerges, and our willingness to peek into a pattern to see what it offers. The outcomes are beautiful patterns, with rarely the same view twice.

THINK ABOUT IT . . .

Here's your next set of questions. These, like the ones in the first chapter, ask you to think about your attitude toward a number of career mobility ideas. Find an opportunity to talk about one or more of these questions. What effect would your answers have on your attitude toward career mobility?

* Which basics of a kaleidoscope view will be easiest for you to put into play? Which will be most difficult?

  - Appreciate patterns

  - Encourage optionality

  - Balance money and meaning

  - Lose the org chart; build an orb chart

* Which of the basics is countercultural for you? For your organization?

* Which do you hope *your* manager will use?

* What opportunities are presenting themselves right now?

* Money aside, what else motivates you?

. . . TALK ABOUT IT

CHAPTER

3

Leave
the  behind

Opportunities still exist . . .

they may even be

MORE PLENTIFUL,

We've said that opportunities still exist . . . they may even be more plentiful. They may just look a little different.

An old management saying goes "You need the right *person*, in the right *place*, at the right *time*."

We are suggesting a change to that saying. What if there were more *right places*? More right places mean more opportunities to grow and develop. It's happening now in organizations where career mobility is taking hold. So our update of the phrase would be "When more *right places* are named and visible, more *right times* will be available to accommodate, engage, and retain *all* the talented *right people* throughout the organization." An inclusive environment, where everyone has growth opportunities, can take hold and flourish in your workplace, too.

Career mobility patterns are flexible. Like the small, colorful beads in a kaleidoscope, which tumble and reshuffle, development experiences can happen in different sequences tailored to individual preferences, abilities, timing, and tastes. When a slight change—a twist of the kaleidoscope—happens, new patterns and possibilities surface. When you want to know your options, you can twist the tube to see what emerges. Or, let's face it, sometimes that kaleidoscope may be shaken by external forces. A merger or reorganization can produce a whole new landscape of possibilities. We need to adjust our vision to see not just the ladder but also the adjacent possibilities.

Regardless of how the patterns come to be, they will be combinations of the six experiences—enrichment, exploratory, lateral, realignment, vertical, and relocation experiences—that we introduce in the following chapters.

Grow Here

You can make a current job more interesting and challenging through **enrichment**. You can grow in place right where you are. All it takes is a very small twist of the kaleidoscope. Shift some tasks. Take on others. A small shift can transform the current job into a learning lab. Specialists build entire careers from patterns of enrichment experiences. They get better and better at what they do and deepen their contributions along the way. **Ask yourself what you learned this week or this month. You might be surprised.**

Try before You Buy

You can think of the **exploratory** experience as a chance to investigate possibilities. It may involve short-term work assignments or shadowing someone who's in a position you may be considering. The exploratory experience could be as simple as having a conversation about the requirements of a role that seems attractive to you. It's a chance to check things out to see what will work—and what might *not* work. Exploring is a very smart step to take before investing time and energy in pursuing other experiences. Exploratory can be a bridge from enrichment to any of the other experiences. **Think about an assignment that intrigues you. How could you learn more about it?**

Sideways to Highways

Lateral experiences usually mean pay doesn't change. Status and scope of responsibility are typically the same or similar. New perspective is the payoff from a lateral experience. When you take on a role in another function or department, you get to view your responsibilities and the organization through a new lens. Lateral experiences can help you to fine-tune skills, build new relationships, learn a new or different approach, acquire deeper hands-on expertise, see the organizational operations from a different angle, and add to your knowledge base. **What sideways options could offer you a new view?**

Step Back for a Reason or a Season

People sometimes choose to **realign** or step back to refocus. Maybe the current job was just not a fit and you're brave enough to admit it. Maybe this step opens a whole new vista that seems exciting, in a part of the organization that's new or growing. It

When more **right places** are named and visible,

more **right times** will be available to engage and retain

all the talented **right people.**

can also be about finding a role that is less demanding, more enjoyable, and better aligned with personal priorities. With the ever-increasing focus on work–life balance, a realignment move is sometimes based on a personal need that, if ignored, might result in a resignation and exit. Realignment usually means letting go of certain responsibilities, time commitments, and, potentially, salary. Whatever the reasons, it is a valid, important option. **Have you ever had to take a step off the treadmill for some reason?**

When Up Is the Way

As we've said, the ladder hasn't completely disappeared. The rungs aren't *all* gone. For some people, a **vertical** move absolutely makes sense. When it works for the organization and for the individual, a vertical experience should definitely be included in the pattern. Vertical moves can bring with them many of the traditional symbols of success, such as titles and monetary compensation. A vertical experience could mean leading a team or project and taking on a more visible role. In reality, it can also come with headaches, so careful thought about when, if, and how a vertical experience would fit into your career pattern is essential. **How will you know when or if a move up is right for you?**

Is That Grass Really Greener?

There's always a way out. The exit door is always there. **Relocation** means leaving for an entirely new organization or industry. It's awkward and sometimes really tough to acknowledge this one. But, alas, it is real. And every person knows the option to step out the door is there. In the past, however, once the door closed, it locked. Today, it's exciting to see how many who leave are welcomed back when they decide to return. And they bring a wealth of new knowledge with them. Some of our clients use the label "boomerang employee" with pride. **What are some signs that it might be time to look outside your current organization for your next growth opportunity?**

Go for It!

The chapters that follow define each of these six experiences. You will find ideas about how to think and talk about them—how each experience might fit into a current or future career pattern.

Before we dive into each of the six experiences, we have a few suggestions for getting started.

First, examine how to grow through **enrichment** experiences. What can you learn right where you are?

Next, use **exploratory** experiences to test other roles and examine other functions or areas.

Enrichment and **exploratory** experiences carry low risk and can be great ways to learn and grow without physically moving to a new area or a new job. They open up multiple alternatives and often can be done while still committed to the demands of the current job. Both can lead to any of the other experiences.

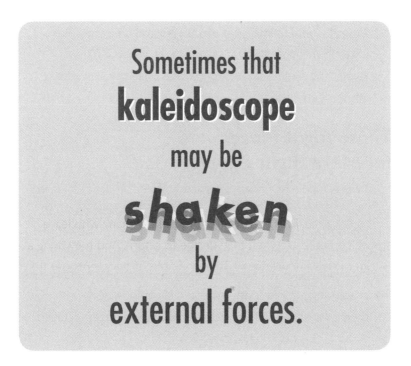

Sometimes that **kaleidoscope** may be **shaken** by external forces.

When you are ready to create your pattern, examine **lateral**, **realignment**, **vertical**, and, yes, even **relocation** experiences to build unique and flexible career mobility patterns. What possibilities are adjacent to what you are doing right now? Should the next experience be **lateral**? Does it make sense to plan a **realignment** in another function in order to switch disciplines? Should a **vertical** experience appear in the pattern? If so, when? And where? Is it time to consider **relocation**? It's your pattern. It's your career.

Remember that this approach is what we *suggest*, but ultimately the selection and placement of the six types of experiences is up to each individual. Careers are made up of multiple experiences creating a unique pattern that belongs solely to the individual.

> Is this description of options just putting rose-colored glasses on a nonpromotion? No, it's not. We have met countless people who shifted their gaze from the job in their telescopic view to consider an option they had never even noticed before, and it changed the course of their careers for the better. Many of them report that they're glad they abandoned the single-minded quest for the job in the telescope. They found a job—a career—that they loved, thanks to appreciating the kaleidoscope.

Those Right Places for More Right People

So, there *can* be many more times and places for all the talented people in any organization. Taking a broad and flexible approach to career growth is key. Adopting a career mobility mind-set that views change as opportunity can open entirely new landscapes for development. Inclusive and widespread talent development results from supporting career patterns that include interfacing with new colleagues, reporting to new leaders, moving from team to team, and learning how differently we all operate. Imagine how much more plentiful growth opportunities could be if individuals appreciated and planned these experiences.

THINK ABOUT IT . . .

Think about *your* career journey so far and the career pattern you are creating for yourself.

* Which of the six career experiences have been a part of your journey so far?

  - **Grow Here** Enrichment

  - **Try before You Buy** Exploratory

  - **Sideways to Highways** Lateral

  - **Step Back for a Reason or a Season** Realignment

  - **When Up *Is* the Way** Vertical

  - **Is That Grass *Really* Greener?** Relocation

* What experiences best prepared you for your current position?

* Which experiences do you hope to include in your pattern, going forward?

* Which experiences are within reach? Which ones seem like a stretch for you?

* Which experiences might match your three mirrors?

* Which experiences do you want to include in upcoming career conversations?

. . . TALK ABOUT IT

GROW
here

Standing still is FALLING BEHIND.

Enrichment is mandatory.

There! We've said it! And growing in place is, in fact, mobility in a world where standing still means falling behind. We need more people who fall in love with what they do, becoming specialists by deepening their abilities and setting the bar higher in their fields.

How many jobs are exactly the same as they were a year ago, or even a month ago? Keeping up with change is a demand in every industry. Yet mind-sets are not changing as fast as jobs are changing. We need to change the conversation. We need to see the current job as fertile soil for career growth.

Every year, individuals who have been raised with technology at their fingertips since they were in their cribs join the workforce and the consumer market. This latest group is equipped with a level of intuitive digital knowledge and familiarity that drives organizations to evolve quickly and constantly. At the same time, employees expect and need the latest technology and tools to do the job.

Those are the internal pressures for change. Externally, customers demand newer and better products. Competitors continually raise the bar. Jobs themselves evolve and the skill sets required to do them shift and change. When we understand this reality, anticipate what's coming, and prepare for it, we're building resilience and readiness to take on whatever comes along.

Growth on the current job can and should happen in every role or assignment throughout a career. Through enrichment, individuals feed their passion about the work, stretch to build new capabilities, and grow professionally.

Enrichment can also be the spark that reenergizes a job that's lost its appeal. Enrichment can rekindle passion and excitement around the work—passion and excitement that may have disappeared beneath daily tasks and deadlines.

So, what can you do to fuel continuous growth or jump-start a job that's gone flat? It's bigger than a learning event. Sure, compulsory

MOBILITY MOMENT

The Sludge Guy

Lynn has a relative who's an environmental engineer specializing in managing wastewater. During his career, he steadily and deliberately deepened his expertise in his chosen field. As the kaleidoscope turned and environmental issues shifted, he further refined his view to become one of the country's go-to guys on sludge.

Did he plan this from the outset? Did he say early on, "Hey, I want to be the sludge guy?" No, but he loves where he is. He proudly identifies as the sludge guy. When you know more about your specialty than most people, you have many chances to contribute and leave your mark. The corporate ladder didn't interest him. He stayed right where he was and created a pattern full of enrichment experiences.

We need to see
the current job as
fertile soil
for career growth.

courses to maintain certifications or meet regulatory requirements are necessary, but enrichment doesn't begin and end in a class-room or webinar. Seek multiple ways to keep growing. If you are feeling burned out, or if someone you know has "retired in place," enrichment can be the ticket to reviving interest and enthusiasm for the work. And everyone needs to master and excel at *the now* before moving on to *the next*.

Take the Change Challenge

Perhaps the easiest way to start a conversation about an enrich-ment experience is to consider a small change or two in the current work scene.

Review the **Change Challenges** that follow and select the questions you want to build into your conversation. Think about the current role, how it's changing or will change in the future. Pick questions that are appropriate to the situation. Dialogue triggered by these questions can uncover multiple ways to maintain engage-ment and keep everyone growing.

CHANGE . . .

. . . WHAT!

A small change in the current tasks can make all the difference.

➤ When you consider the current job, what tasks could be/should be eliminated?

➤ What could be modified?

➤ What could be traded?

➤ What could be added?

. . . HOW!

The approach can open the door to learning more.

➤ Which work processes are draining or demotivating?

➤ What is under your control to change, but that you have never considered?

➤ Where do you need support?

➤ What tasks or process could be completed more quickly or more efficiently?

. . . WHERE!

A switch in the physical surroundings can offer a fresh view.

➤ What other venues could work?

➤ Is working from home an option?

➤ Is working alone or in a team preferred?

➤ What about working at another site? Another city? Another country?

➤ What would the perfect work space look like?

. . . WHEN!

Flexible schedules sometimes make work "work."

➤ When is energy highest?

➤ When is availability to others a must?

➤ When is the best time for solitary work?

➤ When is access to physical resources, tech assistance, or colleagues critical?

. . . HOW MUCH!

Small adjustments can bring better balance.

➤ Looking at the current workload, what do you want to do less of? More of?

➤ What could you delegate? What do you simply want to let go of?

➤ What do you want to keep?

. . . WHO!

Collaborating with great peers can make work interactions an energizing part of the day.

➤ Who do you interface with in a typical day?

➤ Who is a great working partner?

➤ Who simply demands too much of your time?

➤ What relationships are the most energizing? Working with colleagues? Clients? Other departments? Senior leaders? New hires?

. . . WHY!

Meaning and purpose are powerful sources of energy.

➤ How do you feel about the contribution you are making?

➤ When do you know you are making a difference?

➤ How does your work help you address things that are important to you?

➤ How do the organization's values align with what's important to you?

MOBILITY MOMENT

An Enrichment Question Can Change the Whole Conversation

Bev was meeting in New York with senior leaders of a large finance organization. The group wanted to launch a career development initiative in response to a recent survey. The "lack of time" discussion was on the table. One senior leader asked, "If you could just offer us one question to ask—one question that would unlock a career conversation, a question we could encourage every manager in our entire organization to use—what question would it be?"

Bev responded, "If every manager could look into the person's eyes (even via Skype) and ask each direct report, **'What talent do you have that I may not be aware of, that you would love to use more?'** That would be one perfect question."

There was a hush at the table as the leaders looked at one another. Seemed simple enough! One leader suggested they try it right then and there. Each senior leader turned to a colleague and asked about a talent they had that the organization did not know of or was not using. This group, which worked together on a regular basis and felt they knew one another very well, was amazed by what they learned. The energy in the room was palpable—all generated from one simple but powerful question!

Commit to an Enrichment Workout

Just as with the latest news on keeping in shape, this workout doesn't have to take a huge chunk of time out of a busy day. The warm-up questions in this workout can help you choose an enrichment experience. To remember these, think basic calisthenics.

	Reach up	What is something managers do that you've always wanted to take on?
	Reach out	What is something a colleague is currently doing that you would like to learn?
	Reach down	What are you willing to delegate that not only would give you some space but also would open up a learning opportunity for one of your colleagues?
	Reach to the side	What ability do you have—something that comes easily to you—that you could teach, train, or mentor others in the group to do?

Enrichment
can also be the **spark** that
reenergizes
a job.

These workout questions will stimulate enrichment ideas for you or someone you are working with. See if you can provoke the response "I never thought of it like that before."

Growing in place—finding ways to stretch and learn right where you are—can be liberating and even exhilarating. Enrichment experiences keep you fresh, up to date, and learning. A career pattern with multiple enrichment experiences demonstrates an awareness that jobs evolve. Career resilience depends on keeping up with what's needed right now and being ready for what will be needed tomorrow.

THINK ABOUT IT . . .

Answer one or all of the following:

* Pick the change challenge that most appeals to you and spin it out in your imagination. Who can you have a conversation with to take it further?

* Go ahead, pick another challenge and another conversation partner—talk it out.

* What one workout question would help you think about enrichment right now?

* If you had a two-week sabbatical to study an area of interest, what would it be?

* What talent do you have that your manager may not be aware of, that you would love to use more?

* What would you consider your specialty to be?

. . .TALK ABOUT IT

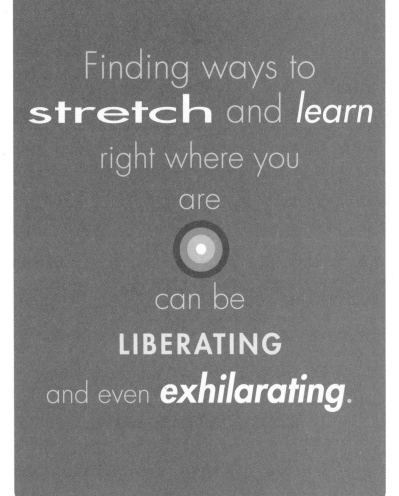

Finding ways to
stretch and *learn*
right where you
are

can be

LIBERATING

and even ***exhilarating***.

CHAPTER

5

Try before you buy

EXPLORATORY

Informed choices beat
bad decisions
all the time.

What's the biggest purchase you've ever made?

Maybe it was a car or a home or a major appliance. It would be hard to imagine driving that car off the lot without reading all you can about it, or at least sitting in it or taking it for a spin.

We probably would not schedule delivery of a new refrigerator without first making sure those shelves will accommodate that five-gallon water pitcher. We watch potential buyers on real estate shows decide not to take a risk after walking through a few rooms or peering into closets. And yet, too often we see employees leap into a new role without considering all the implications—without investigating possibilities—without an **exploratory** experience or two.

Taking on a new role or responsibility without doing the homework can increase stress. Learning more about a role will identify

Exploration is an
elastic experience
that
stretches or contracts
based on interests.

MOBILITY MOMENT

Not My Dream Job

Exploring can be life changing. Lynn has a friend who explored her "dream job" by filling in for two months while a colleague was on medical leave. The experience changed her perspective radically. Not long after taking on the temporary role, she realized that the day-to-day reality of the job did not match her "dream" of it. Other roles would be much closer to matching her three mirrors of skills, interests, and values. After welcoming her colleague back from leave, she promptly dropped that job from her career pattern and added a few more exploratory experiences to broaden her options. She had peered into the kaleidoscope and rejected a view she thought she would welcome.

opportunities that would be a great fit. It can also eliminate others from consideration, or at least place them in the "not so great" or "maybe later" categories. Exploratory experiences can bring development plans to life by providing a road map of behaviors to acquire or polish in order to be seriously considered for a future role. We have all known colleagues who took on leadership roles, only to discover that managing people was *not* their favorite thing.

New functions, expanded markets, and innovation teams are forming and reforming at breakneck speed. All are ripe with learning opportunities and may look enticing. The key is to find the right ones . . . the opportunities that fit interests, skills, values, and aspirations.

Tailored to Fit: Small, Medium, Large

Here's the punch line about exploration: it's an elastic experience that stretches or contracts based on interests. It also gives you a safety net. You can return to home base after the experience with the newfound understanding you need to make informed decisions and choices.

It's easy to get started. Here are a couple of steps to take.

Open the investigation by asking:

- What areas interest you?

- What functions or departments do you want to check out?

- What roles are you curious about?

Build a plan by asking:

- How can you find answers?

- What resources can you use?

- What help do you need?

Exploratory experiences lead to better career mobility decisions.

Encourage multiple "try it before you buy it" experiences. There is a wide range of options within the exploratory experience. Selecting the right ones depends on the focus of your investigation, the nature of the information you want, the degree of detail you're seeking, and the availability of resources and connections.

Here are three categories to help you plan.

SMALL AND SIGNIFICANT: GATHER INFORMATION

Small but significant exploratory experiences take very little time. Some can be accomplished without leaving the current job or even stepping away from the desk! Brainstorm ideas for gathering the information you want. Some useful and speedy ways of info gathering include:

- informational interviews with subject matter experts;

- role and job family descriptions;

- company intranet sites and blogs; and

- internal newsletters and updates.

Encourage multiple "try it before you buy it" experiences.

If you have never conducted an informational interview, use the questions provided in the blue box to prepare.

Informational Interviews

Information gathering through interviewing can be a terrific way to learn more and to gain some exposure in areas outside the team or department.

Prepare by creating an interview questionnaire that can be used almost anywhere. Some questions that uncover important factors include:

- What do you need to know to hit the ground running in this role?
- What are the top five must-have skills for success?
- What does the future look like for your work? For the area?
- What best prepared you for this role?

Informational interviews are opportunities to exercise curiosity, assertiveness, and inquisitiveness and to gain exposure to those who may be hiring in the future.

MEDIUM AND MEANINGFUL: WITNESS THE ACTION

Exploratory experiences may take you away from the job briefly. The trade-offs are worth it, though. Employees who complete exploratory experiences return with a deeper understanding of another area or position. They build a greater awareness of how their work impacts others.

Medium-size exploratory experiences can include job shadowing, focused observations, cross-functional meetings, town halls, webinars, and more.

To support medium-size exploratory experiences, managers may need to make connections with other groups, find coverage for the time the employee will be away from the job, and have conversations to clarify what will be learned from the experience. In addition to technical answers, watch for the following:

- Surprises—what happened that was unexpected?

- Delights—what seemed most promising about the role or function?

- Concerns—what was discouraging or made you pause?

- Skills—what capabilities are must-haves to succeed in the explored role?

Exploratory experiences can offer insights into the daily tasks of a role or function. Those insights are critical to making informed career mobility choices. Whether you come away from the experience fired up about an area or ready to look at other options, you have more information to help you create your career pattern. And you have added to your network of connections.

BIG AND BOLD: TRY IT

Big and bold exploratory experiences usually take you away from the current role for more extended, but temporary, periods. Some of the most common experiences in this category include:

Cross training	Job rotations	Task exchanges
Mentoring	Project assignments	Off-site conferences
Sabbaticals	Vacation/absence coverage	Seminars

While big and bold experiences may require investments of time and sometimes money, the payoffs can be considerable. Employees return with a richer understanding of the organization and better

MOBILITY MOMENT

If Only I Had Known

During a career coaching session, an operations leader who had responsibility for more than 1,500 people told Lindy that he really hated the job and longed to return to being an individual contributor. He dreaded delivering performance reviews, and the responsibility for such a large operation weighed heavily on his shoulders. He eventually found a way to do just that. Through connections with a few former colleagues, he found a role in a small start-up group where he could share his wealth of knowledge but leave the top roles to others. A few solid exploratory experiences early on could have saved him a great deal of angst and also saved his organization from the churn that results whenever a senior leader departs!

information for evaluating their career patterns. They bring back and incorporate into the current role the skill sets they developed elsewhere, thus expanding their own and their team's capability.

Informed Choices Beat Bad Decisions Every Time

Exploratory experiences provide opportunities to gather information, network with new people, and validate or disprove assumptions—all leading to better career mobility decisions.

Yes, there will still be a few bad decisions. Every career pattern includes a few of those. And we learn from them as well. But by selecting pattern pieces that allow for exploring, you can avoid uninformed choices and perhaps a few of those bad decisions.

THINK ABOUT IT . . .

What might exploratory do for you?

* If you had a week to explore any area of the organization, what would it be and why?

* Are there three people who would have insights to share regarding your exploratory interests? Could you talk to one . . . or to all three?

* If you could choose any person to shadow for a day, who would it be and why?

* What would be fun to learn and why? How could you learn it?

. . . TALK ABOUT IT

CHAPTER
6

Sideways to HIGHWAYS

Be open to **alleyways**

you didn't **imagine**

for yourself.

Do you know how to do everything your teammates can do? If you traded places with a peer in another group, could you hit the ground running?

Teams are everywhere, in every industry and every organization we work with today. Movement among teams is more fluid than in the past and offers terrific opportunities to grow. **Lateral** experiences build breadth of expertise—something senior leaders need and value. The person who gets hands-on experience in multiple areas learns functional interdependencies and gains a deeper understanding of just how the organization works.

Years ago, lateral moves carried a subtle warning message. In fact, the accepted political whisper was that if your organization moved you laterally more than three times, they were sending you a coded message that your career was going nowhere! Lateral experiences no longer carry that message. Sideways moves no longer sideline talent. Instead, as the title of this chapter suggests, lateral moves can lead to bigger and better opportunities. People who can fulfill multiple roles build resilience and position themselves as valuable resources in a changing environment.

Picture that kaleidoscope we talked about earlier. To change a kaleidoscope pattern, the beads in the tube shift by a turn of the tube to the left or the right. And that movement, however slight, has a tremendous effect on what we see. Career patterns can transform in the same way, through even small moves to the left or to the right. Moving to the left or the right can expand capabilities and multiply opportunities for growth.

Fit to a T

IDEO, a leading global design firm headquartered in San Francisco, views intense cross-disciplinary project work as core to innovation. Other organizations have capitalized on IDEO's idea of developing the "T person." This individual has more than just depth of

MOBILITY MOMENT

Move Over

During interviews we conducted while writing this book, we asked people to share their feelings about lateral career experiences. We heard about expanding breadth of expertise and learning about different areas of a business or industry. One answer stood out for us, however. One individual shared that, when she looks back on her career, she now realizes how quickly the time passed. She offered this advice to those just starting on their career patterns: "Don't become married to just one path. Be open and explore alleyways you didn't imagine for yourself." In her journey, moving laterally several times enabled her to gain hands-on experience, using skills and developing capabilities that she would have missed had she proceeded straight up the rungs of an organizational ladder.

LATERAL EXPERIENCES
build breadth of expertise—
something senior leaders **need** and **value**.

knowledge (the stem of the T) in a discipline or expertise. They also have a solid grasp of cross-functional systems (breadth), connections, and collaborative skills—adding the top line that makes a T. This combination of depth and breadth enables them to reach across boundaries and address issues that require a broader view. These individuals often step in as the innovators and systems thinkers within an organization.

Lateral moves feed the appetite of T talent by offering chances to broaden understanding, diversify knowledge of the organization and the industry, and practice those collaboration skills. Oh! And lateral experiences don't hurt visibility, either! In fact, people who choose purposely and plan fully to have lateral experiences create new ways to market their personal brands and grow a solid network of connections.

But Wait! Why Should I Do This?

Sometimes, the most challenging part of planning lateral experiences is uncovering and examining what's holding you back. Some thoughts that get in the way are discussed here—with ideas for rethinking each one. See which ones might be standing in your way. Read through the responses and watch for at least one *I never thought about it like that before* in your thinking.

WAIT! WHY SHOULD I?	WELL, HOW ABOUT THIS?
I already do that in this job!	This one is true—sort of! Moving sideways may mean taking on a role that is very similar in many ways to the job you're leaving. That is actually the beauty of the option. Taking transferable skills along enables you to hit the ground running. You have a chance to leverage what you know, broaden your reputation for performance, and focus on areas you want to polish.
It would be like starting from scratch!	Yep! This one is sort of true, too, but mostly in terms of relationships. Sure, there may be some skills to learn and new processes and practices, but the most significant change we hear of from people who make lateral moves involves joining a new team of colleagues. Organizational success depends heavily on relationships and interpersonal skills. Demonstrating an ability to work with a variety of teams and individuals throughout the organization is critical to career success. A lateral experience is a great way to build, polish, or demonstrate that capability.
I just got comfortable here!	Typically, when we feel we've mastered the skills needed and we're performing at a high level, we feel like we are, to use a sports term, "in the zone." We feel comfortable. Difficulty arises, though, when we get too comfortable. Settling into a warm comfy pillow of a role creeps dangerously close to the step just below satisfaction—a sort of sleepy stagnation that thwarts growth. Comfort isn't all bad, but the antennae need to be up to detect when a move to another role could create just the right amount of energy. Daniel Pink calls it "productive discomfort." A lateral experience might be just the ticket that triggers curiosity, stimulates learning, and keeps us fresh. As the kaleidoscope twists, what is comfortable today may be totally different tomorrow.

It won't help me advance my career!	Possibly . . . but most likely, if you give it a chance, it will! More and more senior leaders are very interested in how an individual handles a lateral assignment. Are you able to step into the new job easily? Do you interact with new colleagues with ease? Even if you don't gain more power through the move, you gain experiences that only come from seeing the world through a different lens. Keep track of these experiences and the insights you gain. They will provide you with powerful stories during future interview conversations.
I won't make more money!	This is usually true, though not in every case. If money alone is what you're after, the lateral experience may not be the way to build up your finances. However, if you're looking long term, a series of learning-filled and network-laden lateral moves will up the monetary ante later. If lateral experiences cultivate your skills and abilities, you are positioning yourself for opportunities that surface in the future.

It's perfectly understandable for these objections to exist. It's important to think through how the responses above might help you view lateral experiences in a different light. We recognize that it may not be politically correct to voice them as openly as we just did. In a conversation about lateral possibilities, a brave leader might just give voice to those thoughts by asking, "What are you thinking? How would a lateral experience work for you?" Having the courage to put reservations on the table openly and honestly just may result in one or more of the *I never thought about it that way before!* ahas.

Organizations are clearly moving toward more and more horizontal movement. Conversations that examine the value of lateral experience might be the first step toward shifting a mind-set and making sideways moves career advancing and enhancing.

MOBILITY MOMENT

What Goes Around Comes Around

A manager Bev met on a plane told her this story:

An employee of mine—someone I really liked—offered to help another function of the company. The function needed her specific skill set. I told her I didn't mind as long as she continued to meet her goals in my department. We arranged for her to spend 20 percent of her time with the other function and the remaining time working in her current job. It felt like a win–win. She would get development and the other function would get the help they needed.

In the end, she found she so enjoyed the other role that she did not want to return. Of course I was sad to lose her, but I knew it was the best move for her. And I knew I would eventually find a replacement. As it turned out, in just a few weeks the manager in the other function recommended someone who was the perfect replacement! So it was even more of a win than I expected.

Are We Selling Laterals?

Here's a new way to look at lateral experiences. And it's not just an attempt to make something undesirable look better. It *is* about having a full appreciation for what a sideways move could provide.

Maybe "over" is the new "up." In fact, many studies report that people are in search of personal growth opportunities that promise purpose and fulfillment—the money-and-meaning balance—and not necessarily just a promotion or a bigger pay-check. Here are some truths that we found, and questions you can use to generate conversations about lateral experiences.

THE TRUTH	START A CONVERSATION BY ASKING . . .
Laterals can be a move from no growth to high growth. When the writing is on the wall, indicating that a part of the organization may be heading for downsizing or stagnation, a lateral experience may be the route to an area that is growing.	*Where do you see higher growth possibilities?*
Laterals help build marketability. The more you learn to pinpoint specific assignments that build a well-rounded résumé, the more lateral experiences make sense. Lateral moves provide learning opportunities and can generate or regenerate energy and excitement about the work.	*What skills would help prepare you to achieve longer-term aspirations?*
Laterals can connect employees to new leaders. When you move laterally, you also increase your exposure to new bosses, new colleagues, and others who can help you navigate your career. The more connections you have throughout the organization, the better.	*What leaders and managers would you like to learn from?*

Laterals bring professional challenge.

A high-growth opportunity that fits the kind of challenge you want—a once-in-a-blue-moon type of opportunity—can come through a lateral move. This is especially important if the current job is a poor fit or if you have mastered the challenges in the current job.

What lateral experiences capture your curiosity?

Laterals can offer better work–life balance.

Sometimes a lateral move can relieve burnout for a time and enable you to concentrate on other, nonwork commitments. Concerns about unhealthy work–life balance, stress, or frustration are flags indicating that the time is ripe for a conversation.

What opportunities in your personal life might a lateral experience enable for you?

Laterals help build a portfolio of skills.

Not every role provides the same opportunity to learn or demonstrate skills. When a skill that will be critical in the future is best learned through another role—a role at the same level but in another group—then a lateral experience may be the answer.

What is one skill or competency that you do not yet have but know will be important in the future?

Laterals can help reengage the disengaged.

There is a direct connection between career development and employee engagement (this we know for sure). Bored employees become disengaged quickly. Lateral experiences can overcome boredom by opening up new areas to explore and adding variety that didn't exist before.

What lateral experiences would challenge you (in a good way!)?

Lateral experiences can be routes to promotions.

It's become pretty clear in organizations around the world that flatter structures have done a good job of eliminating many straight-up rungs on the ladder. We need to be reminded that lateral moves (if carefully chosen) can provide specific experience that paves the way for the eventual upward move.

How could a lateral experience be a stepping stone to a future goal?

Of course, as with any options, there are cautions about lateral experiences. Organizational grapevines can be skewed against this opportunity, even if you select it as best for your career pattern. Accepting a lateral opportunity without having passion or interest in it can lead to a career dead end. And, quite frankly, every new experience brings the chance of failure. Although many say "Fail first, fail fast, learn from failure," it can also be a stumbling block that is very difficult to overcome. Examine the positives and the downsides. Weigh all the pros and cons and have conversations to determine how and if the pluses outweigh the minuses before making any move. Only you can determine whether an experience is right for your career pattern.

LATERAL EXPERIENCES
create new ways to
market personal brands
and grow a **network**.

MOBILITY MOMENT

When the Rung Disappeared

An operations manager recently shared with Lynn her story about lateral experiences.

Throughout her career, the manager had continuously pursued the next rung on the ladder. The unwritten norm in her organization was that if you didn't move up every couple of years, your career was slipping away. As the company delayered, though, the only opportunities were lateral moves—and even those options were outside of operations. Considering a staff role had never been on her radar. After the pace of operations, areas like finance, marketing, or human resources seemed less than exciting.

However, she took the step sideways. In fact, she took several. And she found that there were whole new worlds to learn. When she eventually accepted a promotion back in operations, she was selected because she now had a breadth and depth of expertise that few others could replicate.

She feels the lateral experiences led her to make decisions in her day-to-day role that are grounded in a broader view of the overall organization. She now has firsthand experience in how other functions operate and what's important to delivering successful results across the departments.

THINK ABOUT IT · · ·

* Have you taken a lateral move in your career? What was the upside? The downside?

* What other areas of the organization could use your current skill set?

* Which of your abilities and capabilities can most easily be applied and/or transferred to another area?

* What gets in the way of considering a lateral move?

* How will you determine whether a lateral experience is right for you?

· · · TALK ABOUT IT

Maybe "OVER" is the new "UP."

Step back
for a **reason**
or a **season.**

RECALIBRATE

rethink

reconsider

REENERGIZE

Let's be clear about what we mean by **realignment**. When you choose a realignment experience, you are *voluntarily* taking a step back or a step down. You are initiating the move with the support of your manager or mentor or coach. Stepping back can be an opportunity to recalibrate, a chance to rethink a route you may have committed to at one point and now want to reconsider. Or you may include a realignment experience in a career pattern as a stepping stone to future opportunities.

If realignment experiences are not common in your organization, it can be puzzling to understand the *why* behind including this option in a career pattern. The realignment experience is becoming more common, though. We have heard from a number of our clients that employees have a wide variety of reasons for choosing a realignment experience. Several interviewees shared with us that they were:

- returning to an individual contributor role after discovering that management was not all it appeared to be;

- taking on an entry-level position in another function or area of expertise, where there might be more opportunities for longer-term growth;

- seeking a part-time or job-sharing schedule to allow more hours for personal responsibilities;

- opting for a less stressful or time-consuming opportunity; or

- learning a skill set that is only used in a lower position.

A **realignment** experience can **rejuvenate** a career that has become *dreary* or M O N O T O N O U S .

And sometimes it's simply needing some space and time to breathe or reenergize.

Too often, the bad press around the idea of stepping back—the chatter, the buzz, the side glances, the assumption that there must be more to it, for someone to make such a move—is harmful and hurts. However, depending on the circumstances, realignment can be just the *right place and just the right time. When you want to shift your career pattern, when you want to twist the kaleidoscope a full turn or two to find something different, taking a step down or back can allow the space to do just that.*

We've seen this scenario play out over and over in technical organizations we work with. Talented individual contributors are promoted into management as a reward or acknowledgment of their expertise but without careful consideration of what's the best fit for them and for the organization. Unfortunately, when it is not the right fit—when the three mirrors don't line up with the new role—the individuals involved often leave rather than speak up.

As we pointed out when we introduced the three mirrors in chapter 2, finding the right fit—matching skills, interests, and values to what we do—is essential to a successful and meaningful career. When that best fit is a lower-level or previous role, the choice can be refreshing, rewarding, and fulfilling.

MOBILITY MOMENT

You *Can* Go Home Again

Bev's husband was a rocket scientist. (Really!) He loved his technical work, loved the magic of equations. And he was really good at what he did. His expertise was noticed and, as a result, he was asked to take on a management role. He said yes, as many technical people do. It seemed like the right thing to do. After a short time managing others, however, he realized that he truly missed the technical nature of his work. Unlike so many others, he admitted it to his own leader. (OK, with a fair amount of coaxing and coaching from Bev!). He was heard. His manager listened. And he was able to return to the technical work he loved.

A realignment experience can rejuvenate a career that has become dreary or monotonous. The physician we met who gave up medicine to become a human resources manager, or the corporate executive who returned to school to study theology, might be extreme cases. Still, even the young man who went from management to part-time phone representative in order to make time for his band tour paints a positive picture of the realignment possibilities.

Does this sound like we are trying to offer a hard sell for realignment?

Actually, what we are selling here is a challenge. We are challenging you to examine your view of realignment. We are inviting you, once again, to say, "I never thought about it like that before."

How do you perceive individuals who opt to step back in your organization?

Let's examine some possible biases. Ask yourself these questions:

1. Do *you* label steps down or back as "demotions"?

2. Do *you* believe choosing to realign will knock an employee permanently off track?

3. Do *you* assume realignment experiences are for those who can't cut it?

If you answered yes to any of these three questions, there's a risk you might be undervaluing or prejudging this experience.

Labels Matter

Pay attention to words that may be sending the wrong message.

First, are all realignments demotions? The word *demotion* carries a negative vibe. It also implies that the individual may have had little or no input into the decision. Language is powerful. Just the simple step of calling a move a realignment rather than a demotion can change the perception.

Let your conscience be your guide: read the following two statements and see if you have different reactions to each.

> Britt is taking a demotion as a next career step.

> Britt chose to refocus as her next step.

Maybe the two statements felt the same. Maybe they didn't. But how you talk about this option can influence the chatter and, most importantly, can support the choice.

- Use synonymous terms like *realign, shift, adjust, switch,* or *balance* to help pave the way and redirect inaccurate grapevine talk. Positive descriptors will reframe the move as a planned, deliberate, and informed choice.

- Talk openly about any concerns you may have regarding the perception of others—the chatter—and discuss ways you communicate to build support and understanding.

Avoid Sidetracks

The second question we asked you to consider was whether you believe realignment knocks a person off track. Again, it's important to remember that we are talking about an employee-initiated option. To be honest, a realignment *could* result in some temporary

How you talk about this option can influence the CHATTER.

stalls, depending on an individual's longer-term aspirations, but built into an overall pattern, the experience can be a *right place* at the *right time*.

When a realignment experience is part of an overall plan—a pattern that fits the needs at the moment or for the future— then the sidetracking risk is diminished. Planning is key to making realignment a successful chapter of a career journey. Candid

MOBILITY MOMENT

Movin' On Back

Lynn stayed after a presentation one day and talked to a senior manager who was stressed over the loss of a talented sales leader. The sales leader's team had regularly exceeded sales quotas and delivered on every stretch goal. Recent events in the sales leader's personal life, though, had made untenable the travel his role required. A step back into a regional sales position could have worked, but he was concerned about how such a move would be perceived, so he chose to leave the organization rather than face anticipated negative comments. As a result, the organization lost someone who could have continued to contribute and possibly could have demonstrated the company's willingness to be flexible and responsive to employees' needs. The chatter hadn't even happened . . . but the perception that it would resulted in an unnecessary upset for the whole team.

conversations about motivations and risks will support making objective decisions and choices, with full understanding of the consequences.

Like other experiences that take the employee away from the current role and team, a realignment choice might result in "out of sight, out of mind." Plan for how to maintain connections. And brainstorm ways to stay informed and up to date with changes, to keep the rest of the career pattern intact.

Dispel the Perception

The final question we asked you to consider was whether realignment is only for those who can't "cut it." This perception is one of the main reasons people are reluctant to seriously consider and openly talk about a realignment experience, even if circumstances make it a top option. Initiate a conversation about reasons for a potential realignment choice. Ask what's making realignment look like a good option right now. When it's clear that you have control over the decision, you know how it will be communicated, and you have the necessary support, you're ready to realign.

A realignment experience can be the *right place* at the *right time* for lots of reasons.

Support realignment experiences through any or all of the following steps.

TALK . . .	through how the decision will be communicated to the team. Revealing highly personal factors is not necessary, but identifying elements of the decision that are appropriate to share, and positioning the move as planned and beneficial, can diffuse some of the perception that the move was not by choice.
PLAN . . .	how to respond to questions about the decision. No one likes to be caught off guard, so a few rounds of "What will you say if asked . . ." can result in positive rather than negative interactions.
DISCUSS . . .	how existing skills and expertise can be applied in the new role. A rich discussion will include appreciation for what's been learned from earlier roles and will set the stage for effective performance in the realignment experience.

A realignment experience can be the *right place* at the *right time* for lots of reasons. If you catch yourself judging the option before understanding the motivations, turn down the volume of those voices in your head and ask questions to learn more. If you hear others evaluating the move based on outdated perceptions or inaccurate information, step in to help reframe the way they view the move. And, in the process, perhaps a few mind-sets about career mobility will be reset. Aim for someone saying, "I never thought about it like that before."

THINK ABOUT IT . . .

* When have you taken a step back or down? What prompted the move? What did you learn?

* Are there realignment options that could open doors for more growth in the long run?

* What realignment moves have you observed others take? How did others perceive the moves?

* How could a realignment experience be communicated positively in your organization?

* How would you position your own realignment opportunity with others?

. . . TALK ABOUT IT

When **UP** *is* the way

Sometimes

the glitter

is all the viewer can see.

When the telescope focuses only on moving up, sometimes the glitter is all the viewer can see. For decades, **vertical** movement was that shiny object. For some, it still is. Promotions can offer status, responsibility, power, prestige, compensation, title, ability to call the shots, and maybe even a coveted parking space. Some promotion seekers are simply hoping that next rung will bring respect, acknowledgment, and maybe a little envy from colleagues.

Traditional definitions of success were often based mostly on upward movement. It was why you went to college or graduate school. It was why you worked those long, tedious days for someone who was senior to you but maybe not respected by you. The reward at the end looked good. For many, that mental image may be hard to erase. And family and friends may be asking, "So when are you getting promoted?"

Rarely does anyone move in a solely vertical trajectory throughout a career, but upward moves are important pieces of many career patterns. In this chapter, we'll take a look at the rewards and the realities of moving up.

All That Glitters

Promotions can be very enticing. When shiny objects blur a clear vision of reality, though, you may need to adjust the focus. If the choice of a vertical experience decision is based solely on skills but fails to consider the mirrors of values and interests, it may be a poor fit and a big disappointment.

Have you ever seen a trailer for a movie and thought it would be a movie you would absolutely enjoy? Sometimes the trailer is right on. You loved the movie. You walked out feeling great. You even applauded at the screen, along with others in the theater. But there are the other times when you walk away saying, "The trailer *was* the movie!" The best scenes were in the previews! You fell for it and you're frustrated. It wasn't at all like they said it would be. You're disappointed and you realize you will never get those hours of your life back! Further investigation can help you avoid being drawn in by short, flashy previews of that next rung on the vertical ladder.

A move up is a big step. It's usually highly visible in the organization, so it's important to be clear about whether it's the *right place*

Rarely does anyone move in a solely

V E R T I C A L

trajectory throughout a career.

and *right time.* When talking about a vertical experience, it's critical to examine both the upsides—and there are many—as well as potential trade-offs. Consider whether the role would adequately reflect the skills, interests, and values mirrors discussed in chapter 2. Talk about how a vertical experience fits into the overall career pattern. Ask questions that shed light on things that may not be as obvious as that parking space and cool new desk. Talking about all career options while considering a vertical move can produce insights and build a deeper understanding of what the step up truly entails. Conversation may validate the choice or, in some cases, redirect the plan.

MOBILITY MOMENT

I've Always Been Ambitious

During an interview for this book, a client shared her story in response to the question *What advice would you give to your younger self?* She said, "I've always been ambitious, always pushing, driving, and focused—maybe overly so—on vertical moves. If I had the chance to give my early career self some advice, it would be that you don't have to accomplish everything at once. Take your time. Just breathe. Careers take decades. In looking back, in my twenties I was really eager and thought I knew everything. In my thirties I realized how much more I needed to learn. And now, in my forties, I feel I've hit my stride. I still ambitious, but not as hyperfocused on just the next move up."

When Money Is *Everything*

We've all heard the phrase "Money isn't everything!" An unvarnished truth, however, is that sometimes—at certain points, under certain conditions—it *is* everything, or at least is a very compelling consideration. There are situations where money is the deciding factor between options. If a significantly larger paycheck is waved before the eyes of someone who is trying to move out of the parents' basement, crawl out from under a massive student loan

MOBILITY MOMENT

Is It Time to Move Up?

During a break in a recent workshop for new managers, a young man approached Lindy with a question: "How can you really know you're ready to be a leader?" Yeah. A big question for a fifteen-minute coffee break! But, while sipping his coffee, he explained that he wanted to make sure his direct reports who aspired to become managers one day would be better prepared for everything it entails than he was when he took the leap. He shared that, although he was doing well now, his first year as a manager was rough. Is anyone ever absolutely certain of the next move? Maybe not. Among the tips Lindy shared over that cup of coffee: Be curious. Ask great questions. Give candid feedback and have honest conversations. Sometimes the best support a manager can provide to someone who is seeking a promotion is to initiate conversations.

It's **critical** to **examine** both the UPSIDES as well as potential TRADE-OFFS.

debt, pay for a son's or daughter's college tuition, or find an affordable option for a parent's eldercare, they will probably take it.

If you are nodding your head and thinking about that talented employee who was stolen away by a competitor waving cash at them, read on.

Let's turn the table a bit: What if money is the *only* reason an employee jumped another ship to join *your* organization? Well, they're on the team now, so the role you can play—whether you manage the person or are a teammate—is to learn more about *all* the factors that are important to that individual, and to help them make the role the best fit for them. Talk about what attracted new teammates to the organization. Have conversations about the skills they bring and what they hope to learn. Engagement is a team sport. Conversations will build a stronger, more cohesive team. Insights from your conversations will help you support one another in current roles as well as prepare everyone to make good choices about what's next.

Now what about that "meaning" factor? We have met hundreds of people whose financial compensation is not astounding and, in some cases, falls far below what many would consider equitable for the work they do and the critical services they perform. Conversations with these people reveal that their overwhelming motivator is often meaning. Doing meaningful work—feeling that

What if
MONEY
is the only rea$on?

their efforts are making a difference to things that are core to their beliefs—is essential for some individuals to make a solid commitment, to give their extra discretionary effort, and to experience a fulfilling career. Believing that meaning is important doesn't mean you need to become a starving artist, but if meaning is at the top of your satisfaction list, you have to seriously examine how and if the financial gain of a promotion will impact your ability to make the differences that are important to you.

Ready? Maybe Not . . .

There is a saying in the American sports lexicon: "Send me in, Coach!" It conjures up the image of an eager, enthusiastic player ready to jump in and save the day. Unfortunately, there are times when a player's enthusiasm outdistances ability. Here's where you can potentially avoid the pain of a mistake, if not a failure. It's all about *feedback*. The trick here, though, is to receive and deliver the feedback without extinguishing the energy and enthusiasm.

Candid conversations that explore the requirements of a promotion and identify gaps can be eye-opening experiences for someone, without resulting in discouragement. The input may not always be what the person was hoping to hear, but it can be a catalyst for self-reflection.

Here are some ways to self-reflect or help someone else examine a potential move up.

MAKE IT REAL	Interview individuals who have moved to positions higher up the management hierarchy to learn about their headaches, surprises, and satisfactions with the choice. Schedule time to talk about what they learned. Uncover any pluses and potential minuses that come with the experience.
PROVE IT	Talk about examples of when, where, and how you have demonstrated some part of what the step up would require. Discuss what it takes to be ready for a promotion and whether that preparation is complete.
GET TO THE BOTTOM OF IT	Ask questions to find out what's to be gained by the move. What's really at the heart of the quest? Are those hoped-for gains realistic?
SHARE YOUR EXPERIENCES	Tell it like it is—and was—in your career journey. When did you make a vertical move that was a good choice, and when did you jump in too early? When was it the wrong path for someone you worked with? What have you been witness to?

Trust is an essential piece of every career conversation. It's important that both parties have each other's best interests at heart. Making objective comparisons between talent and opportunities may be just what is needed. If you are not ready for a move up, or if the person you are speaking with needs more preparation, a candid conversation can shift the focus and result in a positive outcome for the individual and the team they work with. Not being ready for a promotion right now doesn't mean it will never happen. Feedback and conversation can point to the preparation that makes the next opportunity to move up the right one.

Ready? Maybe So . . .

What if you *are* ready? What if you have a good chance of getting the promotion that appears in the pattern? The work is not done. Even if you are qualified, or if the person you're working with is the perfect person for the job, there are still some important things to consider and talk about.

Candidates—even the most qualified ones—need to present themselves well. Marketing yourself is not always a comfortable and natural thing to do, but unless others who will have input into promotion decisions know you and know what you can do, you may be overlooked. Draw on connections to spread the word. Look for opportunities to share your aspirations with colleagues. If someone on your team would be a great choice for an open position, advocate for them. Share your observations with others.

All done? Almost. Conversation can also help by generating insights through questions. Here are some to get that going:

- Is this the first time you will have direct reports? What will that be like?

- Will you be managing people who are currently peers? How will that impact your relationships?

- In what ways might the move up result in greater dependence on your interpersonal skills and less on your technical expertise?

- What will this change mean for you personally, professionally, and financially?

- What challenges will you face? How will you handle them?

- What concerns do you have?

- What do you most look forward to about this experience?

MOBILITY MOMENT

Can You Say No?

Bev was conducting a workshop at a Women in Leadership conference. The conference was for high-potential women from a wide variety of global organizations. All six mobility experiences were being discussed. When it came to vertical mobility, Bev asked the group if they felt they could say no to an offer of a vertical move. This sparked quite a lively debate. About half of the participants said that if they refused a vertical move, their organization would see the *no* as a statement that "I don't want to be on the high-potential track," and the offer would not come again. The other half of the group said that they felt they could actually say no, if they explained their decision thoughtfully. A well-thought-out no, coupled with honest and candid conversation, is imperative, especially if you want the invitation to be offered again.

Management Role: Yes or No?

Powerful, thought-provoking questions will help you thoroughly examine the opportunity. Becoming a part of management is a big step in any career journey. It comes with some stressors and responsibilities that need careful consideration. This conversation is not about discouraging anyone from making that move up, but it is about taking the step with a realistic understanding of what it means. Questions to consider when a vertical move would put you on the management team include:

- What new tasks will be your responsibility? What tasks will you need to leave behind or delegate to others?

- What abilities do you possess that will help you succeed in the role? What will you need to learn or polish?

- What new standards, procedures, and practices will you need to learn?

- How will you build trust with your direct reports and peers?

- What will your leadership style be?

Vertical—Not Dead Yet!

Vertical experiences are not relics of the past. Not completely. Organizations continue to reduce the number of rungs on the ladder in the spirit of efficiency. Belt tightening and minimizing of layers receive a lot of attention, but we still need full leadership pipelines, so upward mobility will always be somewhere in the mix of options. It's important, though, to have a realistic understanding of the availability of the option as well as your readiness to take it on.

The face of management is changing. Interestingly enough, technology not only has changed the way we do business but also has changed the "who" of leadership positions. More than ever, young individuals far from retirement age occupy those roles, and they surround themselves with powerhouse employees of all ages and generations. Their youth creates an environment focused more on collaboration and less on know-it-all-ism. Perhaps this will change the way we see and experience career mobility and career patterns—particularly upward moves—in the future. The mind-set about what management looks like is shifting with each twist of that kaleidoscope.

THINK ABOUT IT . . .

Are you ready to take on more responsibility, wield some more influence, have a louder voice or broader reach? Think about your answers to these questions:

* Besides money and prestige, what can you gain by a vertical move?

* What could the trade-offs be? What would be lost?

* What about a vertical move would fit with or cause conflict with your values? Your skills? Your interests?

* What might be your next, best vertical move?

. . . TALK ABOUT IT

IS THAT

GRASS

really

GREENER?

We've **all** had days. . . .

We've all had days (or weeks) when we were truly dissatisfied with the job. Maybe today is one of them.

It might be a momentary *I'm done here!* reaction to a frustrating task. Or maybe the result of one too many late nights trying to hit a deadline. Or possibly even the result of a neighborhood get-together where the conversation turned to the pros and cons of everyone's jobs and somehow the cons of your job far outnumbered the pros. This wave of emotion typically passes soon after the immediate issue is resolved.

This chapter is about the deeper waves, the recurring waves of dissatisfaction, the waves that drive careful and serious thought about leaving. And not just leaving a team or a function but leaving the organization entirely. **Relocation**, by our definition, means voluntarily walking out the door.

A time comes in all careers when the writing is on the wall. It's time to move on.

When it's clear that relocation is a good fit in the pattern, is the job done? No! There's still important work to be done when someone is thinking about leaving. The objective is *not* to talk anyone out of the decision. It might be the right time and the right place for them to make just such a move. Instead, the aim is to make sure the person has chosen the relocation experience objectively, considering all the implications of moving on.

The approach depends on what caused relocation to show up in the pattern to begin with. Here are three reasons we see most often.

I'm Not Growing Here!

When there's eagerness to learn and a desire to grow but support is lacking, it's tempting to look elsewhere. Here are a few things to do:

- Have a candid conversation about what type of growth would be the most desirable.

- Examine options for learning that are available *inside* the organization.

- Talk about what support is needed but missing.

- If what's missing is actually available inside the organization, talk about how one of the other five experiences—enrichment, exploratory, lateral, vertical, or realignment—might be examined before stepping outside.

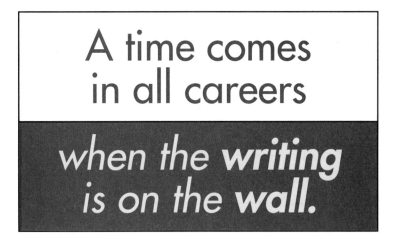

A time comes
in all careers
when the *writing*
is on the *wall.*

MOBILITY MOMENT

Out Is Not the Only Way

Sometimes it certainly looks like there is no other choice than to leave. But we urge you to think again. In the retention research that Bev conducted for a previous book, she interviewed individuals who moved to other companies, and asked why they really left. Most of the people interviewed said they could not have the career they wanted in their current organization. Bev probed further. She asked for the specific opportunity each person wanted. They were always very specific. Then she went back to the original organization and shared with the manager (who had lost the talented person) the specifics of what was wanted. Each time, the manager said, "Why didn't she/he tell me? I could have made that work." What a shame. The sad thing is, all that was needed was a conversation. These conversations can be initiated by the individual or by the manager. The loss is doubled when no one thinks to pursue the real career question.

The fact is that some growth opportunities may *not* be available inside the organization. When that is the case, be open and honest about it—and support the relocation experience through further discussion and planning.

My Best Friend Just Called

Among Gallup's twelve traits of highly productive work groups was one item that raised eyebrows. Item 10 on the list was *I have a best friend at work.* Skeptics questioned whether the "friend" element was really that important. On further examination, though, the finding held up. Loyalty to friends, specifically a best friend, made a difference in retention, productivity, customer metrics, and profitability. So, when friends leave—and call to say they really like their new organization . . . Well, you can see where this is leading.

The answer is not to drop a friend or to change your phone number (although that might be tempting). Instead, talk about:

- **opportunities**—how do the opportunities in a new organization compare with what exists here?

- **connections**—what will it take to rebuild a network of connections in another organization?

- **influence**—how long will it take to establish credibility and have influence in a new place?

- **compensation, benefits, and extras**—how do the new organization's money, benefits, and vacation really compare?

Listen to the answers. Decisions to leave can be risky but also rewarding. It's important to get a clear picture of the risk and reward of the choice.

It's Time! My Next Chapter Is Elsewhere

When it *is* time to go, a smooth exit is the goal. It's not always easy. The departure of solid performers can be painful for everyone involved. Think carefully about three factors that can help you to handle the exit in the best way possible.

Put the key under the mat.

1. THE KEY COULD BE UNDER THE MAT.

Organizations are increasingly open to returning talent (also known as the boomerang theory). There is growing recognition that the expertise and perspectives gained from an outside experience can prove valuable when a former employee steps back through the door. If the organization is open to returns, knowing the door is open may be just the invitation that's needed. We encourage "elegant exits" coupled with "respectful returns."

2. ALUMNI ARE POWERFUL AMBASSADORS.

Whether your organization has a formal alumni group or not, exiting employees who had a good experience in their prior organization can be ambassadors for your brand. One client shared that they recognize some employees will only collect a paycheck from them for a time, but they hope to have those employees as customers for life, or as clients, when they move into roles in a "buying services" organization. Talk about ways to continue to take pride in having worked here. Former employees can be terrific sources of employee and customer referrals. They often become clients or reach back as partners.

3. EXITS CAN ENLARGE THE NETWORK.

When asked what advice she would have for her early-career self, a client shared, "Take care to stay connected to the people who helped you along the way." She regretted losing touch with some talented colleagues she had met in her journey. Talk about how to stay connected to the organization.

Relocation Clues . . . and What to Do about Them

Those three approaches work when you know relocation is showing up as part of a career mobility pattern. But what if you don't know? How can you avoid being blindsided by an unexpected exit?

Here are some clues that something might be happening.

CLUES	ACKNOWLEDGE WHAT YOU'VE OBSERVED AND . . .
Productivity decline could be due to burnout, boredom, or simply a breakdown of commitment.	. . . ask "What's up?"
Disinterest in development may mean opportunities to grow seem out of reach.	. . . ask "What's up?"
Resistance to taking on new tasks could be a sign that more work has become just that—more work!	. . . ask "What's up?"
Frequent private phone calls or hushed conversations could mean a surprise party is in the works! Or it could mean a recruiter is reaching out—or reaching *in*—with enticements to leave.	. . . ask "What's up?"
Value conflict may mean that the employee's values and the organization's values are at odds with one another.	. . . ask "What's up?"

MOBILITY MOMENT

When Fit Is No Longer It

Lynn was working with a client group on career development. The client wanted their employees to assess their overall "career fit" with their role in the current organization. The company was looking to grow significantly over the next three to five years and wanted to make sure they had a truly committed workforce to make it happen.

Lynn noticed one of the participants struggling with the "values" exercise, a cornerstone and first step in the career development process. She approached this person on the break to see if she could offer some guidance. The employee shared that, although it was clear that company growth was part of the organization's vision and strategy, he realized that his number one value was spending time with family and friends. The lightbulb moment for this employee was that, although working long hours and traveling extensively was a part of the job that he had enjoyed over the years, his value system had shifted. It was time for this employee to find a work environment that better supported his own values. As a result of this "discovery," he opted to find a company whose demonstrated value system more closely mirrored his own.

Have a conversation to examine what's behind the clues. If there is a solid level of trust between parties, conversations will be open and candid. If there is limited trust, it may take more than one or two conversations to get this moving in the right direction.

Elegant Exits

When the kaleidoscope reveals a relocation experience that is simply too perfect to pass up, arranging an elegant exit is essential. Ignoring the departure can be more detrimental that the exit itself.

You can make an elegant exit happen. Here's how.

- **Celebrate!** Work to decide when and how you will announce the planned departure.

- **Share the story!** Departures are ripe for rumor. You can avoid that by having an open forum where the team hears what's happening, directly.

- **Talk about it!** Initiate a dialogue with the team about how the departure will impact the work that needs to get done. Discuss input and ideas.

- **Make it a growth opportunity!** Use the upcoming opening as an opportunity for growth for others. Possible short-term coverage assignments or temporary shifts in tasks could be just the right thing for some others on the team.

- **Encourage continued connections!** Talk about how team members can remain in touch after the relocation move is completed.

Honor Respectful Returns

This approach can be a win–win–win. It allows the person to be welcomed back if and when the time is right. It pulls in experience, knowledge, and skills the organization can leverage—and that may

MOBILITY MOMENT

Employee for Now. . . Ambassador for Life

Lindy talks about this one a lot. She believes that no one wants to watch a talented employee or trusted colleague walk out the door. Departures leave holes in the organization, and teams sometimes scramble to manage the loss. More and more, though, employee exits are being viewed as inevitable and maybe not as bad as we thought. Several of our clients have created active alumni groups to keep former employees connected with one another and with the organization. One senior leader, himself a "boomerang" employee, having left and returned three times, points out that an external perspective can add tremendous value to an individual's career journey and to the organization that welcomes him or her back. Returning employees bring new views, fresh ideas, and sometimes a whole new approach and appreciation for how the company operates. Whether someone leaves for a short time or a lifetime, they carry the experience with them. They can become positive voices and enthusiastic ambassadors for the organization, if the exit was an elegant one.

not be available inside. And it demonstrates to others that the organization treated this individual with fairness and respected their decisions and choices.

An organization that encourages open communication about departures is demonstrating that respect, authenticity, transparency, and genuine interest in growth and development are valued here. All are key to building and maintaining a high level of trust among the team.

Talk Now, Not Later

Our retention research shows that stay interviews are more effective than exit interviews. Stay ahead of the curve. Often an exit interview is too little, and way too late!

Most times, conversations conducted at the first hint that there might be something brewing can produce great turnarounds. Think *stay interview* instead of *exit interview.* A person typically checks out emotionally, demonstrating all the observable behaviors—diminished

commitment, declining productivity, lack of enthusiasm, decreasing involvement—well before they decide to physically walk out the door. This gives the proactive, observant leader or colleague a chance to work on finding out what's going on. What's behind the behaviors?

THINK ABOUT IT . . .

Select a few questions to talk about *now*! Don't wait until a relocation experience is in the works. A conversation now might uncover ideas that will keep relocation at bay.

* How have you grown here? What have you learned?

* How have your expectations been met? What surprised you? What disappointed you?

* How would you describe your time here to others outside the company?

* What advice would you give to a new hire in order for him or her to be successful?

* What would attract a "boomerang" employee to walk back in the door?

. . . TALK ABOUT IT

Go for it!

SOMETIMES

it takes *more*

than just wanting

to **do** something.

Throughout this book, we have asked you to view career mobility through a kaleidoscope lens. We have challenged you to create a personal career pattern from six types of developmental experiences. We have offered questions as conversation starters to think about and talk about. And we have encouraged you to have conversations that lead to insights and ideas.

If you are saying "Yes! I can't wait to get started," then maybe our work here is done. But we all know—any of us who have spent time inside busy organizations—that it's rarely as easy as it sounds. Sometimes it takes more than just wanting to do something. Here's what we think it will take for you to seize development.

Courage—to speak from your heart about what you want from your career pattern. It takes courage to give and receive the feedback that shapes development. It takes courage to redirect and let go when things change. Courage empowers you to accept an experience that may not be traditional but that matches your interests, values, and skills. It takes courage to say that your mobility is going to mean growing right where you are for now. It takes courage to be a straight talker with those who report to you. Leaders who beat around the bush and don't give their team members the feedback they need, when they need it, lose the best opportunity for a development dialogue. Encouraging team members to ask for feedback from others, to validate or invalidate one's views, takes courage—on the leader's part as well as the employee's. Sometimes it takes courage to say yes . . . and other times it takes courage to say no.

Commitment—to stay the course and do the work. Yes, development takes work. And change is not always comfortable. Remember that we learn at the edge of our comfort zones. So step to the edge. Keep the dialogue going. Talk about what gets in the way of good intentions. Both sides need to make commitments. Individuals need to commit to following through on their development plans, and they need to speak up when they are sidetracked. And leaders should commit only to something they can deliver. Keep yourself and others on track. Talk about development and have those conversations!

It's time to ask,
Why bother?

Collaborate—to build an adult–adult dialogue. Once upon a time, managers sat down with their direct reports and told them what they thought the next career move should be. Detailed career path charts were provided, showing every gate to conquer. That conversation had a parent–child flavor. Today, the conversation is and should be collaborative. It can be initiated by a leader or by an employee. These collaborative conversations can be with one's own manager or with another person in the organization who has served as a mentor or guide. It can even be with a peer or a group of peers. The secret to any of these conversations is the genuine give-and-take. When two or more people come together for this dialogue, options are bound to multiply exponentially.

Connectedness—to maintain or create the connections you need to support growth. Surprised to see this one in the list? Here's why it's included. Careers don't happen in a vacuum. Careers evolve within workplaces and organizations. The employee–manager covenant is more important than ever. Mentors and coaches, formal or informal, make a difference. Go find them. Connect to the resources you need. Build relationships. Get input, insights, and feedback. Draw on your connections, and reciprocate.

Confidence—to draw on the resources that will enable you to act confidently even in uncertain or ambiguous circumstances. All too often we second-guess ourselves. We want to pursue a certain track but we talk ourselves out of it for any one of a number of the reasons outlined in this book. Instead of moving forward, we overthink. We list the obstacles instead of the opportunities; we don't trust ourselves. Confidence and self-empowerment go hand in hand. The more confidence you exhibit, the more others will follow. Leaders who know how to instill confidence in their teams show respect, give space, and notice when others take chances and risks. They are able to describe what they see and to give it a name. Do you notice when someone on your team takes an uncertain step? Do you notice when you try something different? Double-click on those moments.

Mobility Moments Revisited

The individuals whose stories we have shared as "mobility moments" have what it takes. Some took risks that paid off, and others learned from not-so-successful moves. A few persevered, while a few others wished they had. The support of managers, mentors, coaches, and peers came up over and over.

We can't experience everything ourselves. Learning from others' stories can fill that gap. We hope some of the mobility moments led you to reflect on your own experiences or to ask others about what they have learned in their journeys so far.

So, is that all there is?

Not quite.

It's time to ask, *Why bother?*

Close the Loop

We know even the best ideas can be overshadowed by other pri-orities when reality hits. When you feel your development energy flagging, the following "because" list will help you to recharge.

Because *"more right places" simply makes sense.*

The existence of more right places gives individuals permission to think and act differently. When multiple experiences are celebrated in an organization, individuals have a variety of ways to feel rewarded for good work. The competition for a limited number of coveted positions is lessened. Recognition becomes more inclusive, and managers have additional ways to support the growth of their teams.

Because *everyone wants to succeed.*

No one shows up saying "I hope I fail at this." Solid development plans and career patterns make individual and organizational routes to success clear. Successful organizations are collections of successful people working together.

Because *working with talented, engaged people is awesome!*

Being surrounded by great people, being charged up to do your best, leading yourself and one another to stretch and grow and deliver the best possible future, makes for a pretty terrific experience. Talent stays when the future is hopeful. When it's not, talent walks.

Because *bottom lines matter.*

When people disengage or leave because they aren't growing, it costs money. When talent jumps ship for opportunities that are missing or hidden in the current organization, money that could be spent on improvements and innovation is redirected to recruiting, hiring, and training.

Because *everyone has a career.*

No matter how many years you work, or how many or few jobs you hold, you will one day look back over the days, months, and years you spent working. That view—that pattern—will be the career you created for yourself. You may have had great mentors and managers. You may have had incredible experiences. You may have made some great choices and some poor ones. Regardless, it will be your career pattern. Make it amazing!

Because *it's the right thing to do.*

Helping one another to grow and reach your aspirations is abso-lutely the right thing to do—for you, for your team, for the orga-nization. When people learn and grow and realize their potential, everyone wins. Growth is a basic human need. Survival itself has depended upon learning new ways to do things and adapting to a changing environment. So, yes, growth is basic and essential.

The Kaleidoscope Is Turning Right This Minute

Are you ready for the new view?

With every tiny turn, opportunities change and new possibilities emerge. The reality that people are now responsible to grow their own careers opens up unprecedented opportunities to those who adopt the *Up Is Not the Only Way* mind-set.

Here's your call to action. You now have the following:

Questions to ask and answer

This new mind-set requires asking great questions and listening intently so you can gain valuable insights from all conversations. *Start those conversations.*

Experiences to examine and evaluate

Your career patterns will be combinations of the six experiences outlined in chapters 4 through 9. How they fit together is up to you. Which experiences are next in your pattern? *Create your pattern.*

Your Mobility Moment

We saved this one just for you. If reading this book made you . . .

- think "I never thought about careers that way before," then we are pleased.

- say "I am going to have some conversations about this," then we are happy.

- seize the opportunity and take action, then we are thrilled!

Go for it!

Acknowledgments

Truly, it took a village. We garnered help from many wonderful "villagers" who cared about the authors and the message of this book. Many came to the village square often, to sit by the fire and exchange ideas.

We started with a small team—we three authors and our sales muse, Donna Kohlbacker. With twelve years of experience in our organization, Donna was with us from the start, bringing us stories from the clients she served and helping us to clarify our message. The team grew with the addition of Lindsay Western, our wonderful, tech-savvy MBA student, who challenged us continually from her millennial point of view, with her honest, no-holds-barred feedback.

Ann Jordan, our VP of Product Development, joined at our fireside often. She brought her experience of working on prior books and an ear for listening to the learning tools we would soon begin to think about. We were also lucky to have the magician Nancy Breuer and her "Clear Magic" editing skills. Nancy was able to helicopter up over the entire project and give us clear and workable feedback in the gentlest of ways.

We truly appreciate the support and help from our many colleagues at Career Systems International. Cile Johnson, our VP of Global Sales, challenged us with some great questions. Beverly Crowell, Senior Consultant, added wisdom, and Richard Aldersea, our fearless leader, kept us thinking bigger and better.

Our CSI colleagues, located far and wide, also responded to our calls for mobility moments and helped us stay tuned to the global audiences that would be the readers of this book. They were supportive through thick and thin and always offered advice, counsel, and a listening ear. Lorianne Speaks and Lindsay Watkins were steadfast, helping us to stay continually in touch with one another. Our clients around the globe gave us their time, thoughts, insights, stories, and feedback.

The experience of meeting the Berrett-Koehler team, and presenting to them on our Author Day, was nerve-racking but wonderful. Steve Piersanti was a straight talker from the start and pushed us in ways that we never would have gone. He stretched us and, in the process, our work with him and with his organization became another significant step in our own career development.

Finally, we deeply acknowledge one another. We each brought something so different to the writing team. We realized that we were meant to do this together, because the project demanded that we meld our skills and make this a true learning experience.

Lindy's ability and ease with language, her experience leading a Fortune 100 global career effort from the inside, combined with twenty years of delivering learning solutions from the "outside," gave her a strong hand in conceiving what would speak to readers. Lynn's experience as a senior manager inside another Fortune 100 company enabled her to keep us on a PERT chart track, and her position at CSI as the leader of our team of global consultants kept us grounded in the delivery work we were doing. Bev's never-ending quest to learn more, and to share her learning with us, made our dialogues rich. It also enabled us to be in a state of constant collaboration. Of course, Bev's experience with prior books and her amazing network of friends and colleagues kept our learning on the edge. Finally, her enthusiasm and "Isn't this exciting?" kept us smiling, even when we were all totally exhausted.

FROM BEV

I've had wonderful support through a fantastic network of colleagues, owners, and founders of companies like mine, and longtime girlfriends who continue to nourish me when I'm up as well as when I'm down. (You know who you are!) I also have the support of a wonderful family, my brothers (Alan and Jeff) and their families, and my rocket scientist-turned-CFO husband, Barry. I am blessed with two daughters, Lindsey and Jill, and (my third daughter) Roxy, who, at the writing of this book, is 107 in dog years!

FROM LINDY

Thank you to the many colleagues and friends who helped by reading rough cuts of *Up* and commenting and offering suggestions along the way. And thank you to my husband, Bruce, my sons, Chris and Matt, and my grandson, Seamus, who listened when I was stuck on a word or chapter or deadline and who helped me laugh and relax just when I needed it. And thank you to Bodhi, my four-legged, devoted office companion, all eleven furry pounds of him, for keeping me company during the early-morning rewriting time.

FROM LYNN

Thank you for the love and support of family. My children, Shelbie and Justin, the loves of my life, who have a favorite quote: "Mom, don't use that coaching stuff on us, please." Duly noted. My mom and dad, who were there to listen to my celebrations and tales of woe every step of the way—and loved me just the same. . . . I could not have done it without you all, and I am eternally grateful. Thank you also to the Lunch Bunch, who would challenge my professional (and personal) thinking through the years; my Buffalo and Atlanta friends, who are stuck with me forever (sorry, not sorry); and my CSI colleagues, who have supported this effort throughout. Always appreciated, and never forgotten

Index

meaning
  balancing with money, 17–18
  and purpose, 39
medium and meaningful
  exploratory experiences, 51–52
mentors, roles and responsibilities,
  6–7
mobility moments
  exploratory experiences, 48,
    53
  exploring a dream job, 48
  lateral experiences, 58, 62, 66
  the perfect enrichment
    question, 40
  personal, 116
  purpose of, 113–114
  realignment, 72, 76
  relocation, 99, 103, 105
  the sludge guy, 36
  upward movement, 85, 86, 91
money
  balancing with meaning, 17–18
  as motivation, 86–88
moving to a new location. See
  relocation.

N

negative view of realignment,
  72–74, 76

O

optionality in career paths, 16–17
orb charts, 18–20
orbiting models of work, 18–20
org charts **vs.** orb charts, 18–20
organizations, roles and
  responsibilities, 7
ownershift in career paths, 5–8
owning your career, 4–6

P

patterns in kaleidoscope views,
  15–16
physical surroundings, switching, 38
promotions, 83–85. See also
  upward movement.

Q

questions to ask
  enriching your current
    situation, 40–41
  guidelines for, 116
  informational interviews, 51
  lateral experiences, 62–65
  movement into management,
    92
  realignment biases, 74–78
  self-assessment, 90
  sidetracks, 75
quitting. See relocation.

R

realignment
  biases, questions to ask, 74
  description, 27–28
  mobility moments, 72, 76
  negative view of, 72–74, 76
  overview, 71–74
  planning, 78
  questions to ask, 74–78
  rejuvenating a career, 72–73
  right place, right time, 77–78
  sidetracks, 75–77
  vs. demotion, 74–75
relocation
  alumni as ambassadors, 101
  boomerang employees, 101,
    104–106
  description, 28
  friends as resources, 100–101

About the Authors

BEV

If anyone had told me that I would probably go down in history for just the six words that headline this book, I would never, ever have smiled. Now, I'm smiling. For those of you for whom the title sounds familiar (I know how old you are!), that book (1982, 1997) was based on my doctoral dissertation (UCLA) and presented a systems approach to career development. There was only one chapter that actually talked about this subject.

This is a totally different book. I've learned that my real skill is not in the academics of career development (though all of our work is research based) but in making the complex simple for managers and individuals. In this fast-moving world, the easier we can make our teaching, the more effective we can be.

If luck is where planning meets opportunity, then I've had some great luck. I realized, early on, that I do my best work in collaboration with others—and I found some wonderful and amazing "others" to work with me. I love learning and love finding ways to make that learning easy to remember. I've had the good fortune to build a nourishing network as founder of Career Systems International. Together we turn ideas into practical and engaging learning solutions that have stood the test of time.

I was honored (and tickled) to be awarded the 2010 Distinguished Contribution for Workplace Learning and Performance Award by the Association for Talent Development. (And I was glad to be alive to receive it!) The designation is given to pioneers and prophets who have had enduring impact and influence, originality of ideas, a substantive body of published work, and a contribution that raises the visibility, credibility, and stature of the field.

I do my best writing on airplanes. (My husband offered to buy me a seat belt for my office chair, but that wouldn't be the same!) *Love 'Em or Lose 'Em*; *Love It, Don't Leave It*; *Help Them Grow or Watch Them Go*; *and Hello Stay Interviews, Goodbye Talent Loss* were all done with brilliant and creative coauthors who partnered in every step. I gain my inspiration thanks to decades of work in organizations. In the beginning, I taught workshops in our specialty areas of engagement, development, and retention. Lately, my main work is delivering keynote speeches to client organizations and large conferences around the globe. Every presentation makes me nervous, but every experience provides opportunities for new creative outlets.

The book you hold in your hands builds on thirty-five years of the work of hundreds who have stood before classrooms, and now computer screens. We look forward to adding your insights to this ongoing work.

LINDY

"Never stop learning," a mentor told me, quite a few years ago. I listened. And I am still learning every single day. My career pattern has included all six of the experiences we write about in *Up*. I stepped up and back and over and, at times, chose to grow right where I was. Some experiences surprised me with how amazing they turned out to be. Others that I expected to learn little from—*What on earth could I learn from being a management intern for a finance company, anyway?*—became turning points that led me to twist that kaleidoscope again and again.

I believe that careers don't stop and start. For me, a career is a lifelong journey that may include wildly different types of roles but, in the end, becomes a unique and individual mark on the organizations and people you work with along the way. My journey has taken me inside corporate walls as manager, trainer, human resources professional, and director. From operations roles, I added financial forecasting and budgeting to my skills list, along with change leadership and performance management. When my teaching credentials and deep interest in the learning process led me to the world of employee development, I dived eagerly into instructional design and training delivery. My time as Director of Worldwide Career Development for the American Express Company confirmed my passion for the topic of careers. That role also led me to Bev Kaye—an introduction that evolved into a decades-long friendship and amazing professional adventures. When Bev asked me one of her favorite questions—"What's the one thing you *can't not* do?"—I discovered that my answer was "Career development."

As a Senior Consultant for Career Systems International, I've worked with government agencies committed to their missions and nonprofits devoted to their purposes. I've partnered with leaders to design and implement award-winning programs and initiatives focused on career development and employee

.engagement. My work has taken me to boardrooms filled with senior teams committed to designing powerful engagement strategies, hospital kitchens to meet with employees whose development and engagement is essential to patients as well as the organizations they work for, and to roundtables with military officers focused on coaching and professional growth. I've learned that people around the globe, whether on the manufacturing floor, in an IT think tank, on an aircraft carrier, or at a desk in a corner office, share the desire to have rewarding and meaningful careers. Each experience presented perspectives I may not have considered before and resulted in insights that I could carry to my next assignment.

The opportunity to write this book with colleagues I respect and enjoy was one of those pattern pieces that sparkled when it appeared. Yes, it was work. Yes, it stretched my thinking and sometimes made me wish for more hours in the day. But it has been a labor of love. In the introduction to his book *Your Signature Path,* Geoff Bellman wrote, "Thousands of people have walked this same ground before us, but we each walk it in our own way." My hope is that readers of *Up* will discover ways to make their walks as rewarding and meaningful as possible.

Best wishes for a wonderful career journey!

LYNN

Little did I realize that I would find myself at this place. After many years in the corporate world (GE Capital, GE Aerospace, Martin Marietta, and Lockheed Martin), I have lived the very same career mobility experiences that we talk about in *Up,* without the benefit of the titles or the descriptors that we expand upon here. Although my career began at Capital as a financial analyst for planes, trains, and ships, my passion was always around the human capital side of the equation. My interests, values, and maybe even skills seemed to shine a little brighter around those experiences. At the time, I did not know what to attribute it to; the moves just happened, and they "felt right." Random, or so I thought. Later in my career, my work with Career Systems International as a Senior Consultant took me across the globe, consulting on those similar career development and engagement strategies. Maybe that career pattern was not so random after all. Fast-forward nine years: I loved this work so much that I was honored when asked to come on full time as the Vice President of Quality Delivery, coaching our thirty-plus consultants across the globe, working with their own passions in our space. (The truth is that I learn more from these talented, gifted, inspiring individuals every day than I can ever give back. Thank you!)

Now, as a result of my experiences, I am living that authentic calling: helping others to realize their full potential through our work in coaching and consulting around career development and employee engagement. To write a book on these same subjects, with colleagues whom I admire and respect more than they will ever know, was beyond my wildest dreams. Thank you!

I have been fortunate to work with many great leaders throughout my journey—some who called me a zealot at times (meant as a compliment, I am sure) but, all in all, leaders who were not afraid to tell me the straight truth in the interest of consistently raising my own standard bar. "For that which does not destroy us, makes us stronger" (even if it stings a little). Okay. . . . If they said so, I believed them, and I am grateful—now that I look back.

While traveling through the experiences and patterns we write about in the book, I thought it was just plain luck. However, now that we reflect, it was much more than that. . . . It was willingness to take risks and be flexible, coupled with the safety net of those around me who saw a much bigger picture than I ever could have imagined at the time. The encouragement of one leader to "get that MBA and I will see to it that you get your coveted human resources role" was all that I needed to follow my heart. That one conversation led to a twenty-year "experience" in the

HR field, allowing me to partner with some of the best leaders in the business world, seeing them through mergers, acquisitions, business closings, and many human capital transitions that literally changed lives. Now *that* is the beauty of support, mentorship, and true career advocacy: lifting others up as a result of our own experiences, and paying it forward for the benefit of someone, or something, else. Now I realize that it was a combination of things—diverse opportunities, supportive leaders, well-placed conversations (and feedback), and the willingness to "step out of the box" in order to grow. Now that the descriptors exist in this book, I hope many readers will realize their own potential and passion and give themselves permission to live their wildest dreams.

My best in your kaleidoscope efforts.

CAREER SYSTEMS INTERNATIONAL

Start Talking: Conversations to Develop, Engage, and Retain

Organizations worldwide have achieved powerful and measureable outcomes by delivering Career Systems International's learning solutions. Given our forty-year history of addressing complex issues and applying a practical approach, your leaders/managers and employees will walk away from these experiences and say, "I can do that." Their learning time will be spent on the how-to.

A simple, yet powerful learning element—conversation—is core to all of our areas of practice. Although the act of talking seems simple, the "art" often demands more than a book to bridge the knowing–doing gap. And because we know that discussions take two, both your managers and your employees learn their role in conversations to develop, engage, and retain talent.

CONVERSATIONS TO DEVELOP

Career development consistently ranks as a top driver in employee engagement, not only impacting retention and engagement but also fueling an organization with innovative, productive, and committed employees.

The book you hold in your hands (or are reading on the screen) is based on the belief that opportunities in organizations are plentiful if you are open to all possibilities. The *Up Is Not the Only Way* microlearning solution will help your leaders and employees prepare for and engage in conversations to mobilize action around career choices. Go to www.UpIsNot.com to access Kickstart Mobility; password: upisnot.

With CSI's **CareerPower**® suite, your managers and employees gain the confidence and competence to hold meaningful development conversations, aligned to business strategies. Together they create a culture in which learning and growth are ongoing and organizational talent is optimized.

With *Help Them Grow or Watch Them Go*, you can introduce managers at all levels to a practical approach for this critical dialogue. Embedded in this microlearning solution is the theme that development happens one conversation at a time, over time.

CONVERSATIONS TO ENGAGE

When managers and employees are comfortable with their roles in the conversations, engagement becomes a two-way street. Business results are maximized when both players not only know what to do but also are empowered with the strategies to actually do it.

Your managers gain the experience and knowledge needed to engage their talent. *Love 'Em or Lose 'Em* brings twenty-six low- to no-cost strategies to life as managers learn the principals of engagement, how to converse with all direct reports, and how to create individualized engagement plans.

With *SatisfACTION Power,*® your employees are empowered to create the conditions they need to improve job satisfaction, as supported in the *Love It, Don't Leave It* book. Your employees can take charge of their own engagement by making opportunities to have their job of choice, without leaving for greener pastures.

CONVERSATIONS TO RETAIN

Your managers learn not to wait until the exit interview to understand what employees want, in *Hello Stay Interviews, Goodbye Talent Loss*. The stay interview process is detailed in this micro-learning solution, which is designed to build trust and deepen the connection with employees. Stay interviews are one of the most powerful strategies in a successful manager's playbook.

It's more than learning solutions . . .

You also can access a variety of CSI resources to reinforce and sustain the focus on development, engagement, and retention for the long term. Whether it's building a strategy, fostering impactful communications, training, forming coaching relationships, or simply using part of our library of tools, we have a variety of ways to keep the conversations flowing.

So . . . let's talk!

www.careersystemsintl.com
1.800.577.6916

Facilitator-Led • Virtual Facilitator-Led • Blended Experiences • eLearning Solutions • microLearning • Proctored
Webinars • Keynotes • Train-the-Trainer • Coaching • Consulting • Sustainers • Portals • Libraries • Communications

Berrett–Koehler
Publishers

Berrett–Koehler
Publishers

Connecting people and ideas
to create a world that works for all

Dear Reader,

Thank you for picking up this book and joining our worldwide community of Berrett-Koehler readers. We share ideas that bring positive change into people's lives, organizations, and society.

To welcome you, we'd like to offer you a free e-book. You can pick from among twelve of our bestselling books by entering the promotional code BKP92E here: http://www.bkconnection.com/welcome.

When you claim your free e-book, we'll also send you a copy of our e-newsletter, the *BK Communiqué*. Although you're free to unsubscribe, there are many benefits to sticking around. In every issue of our newsletter you'll find

- A free e-book
- Tips from famous authors
- Discounts on spotlight titles
- Hilarious insider publishing news
- A chance to win a prize for answering a riddle

Best of all, our readers tell us, "Your newsletter is the only one I actually read." So claim your gift today, and please stay in touch!

Sincerely,

Charlotte Ashlock
Steward of the BK Website

Questions? Comments? Contact me at bkcommunity@bkpub.com.

MIX
From responsible
sources
FSC® C113845

Certified

Corporation
bcorporation.net